Smart Love

Other books by Nancy Van Pelt

The Compleat Marriage
The Compleat Marriage Workbook
The Compleat Parent
The Compleat Parent Workbook
The Compleat Courtship
The Compleat Courtship Workbook
The Compleat Tween
From This Day Forward
To Have and to Hold
Train Up a Child
We've Only Just Begun
How to Talk So Your Mate Will Listen and Listen So Your
    Mate Will Talk
My Prayer Notebook
Creative Hospitality—How to Turn Home Entertaining
    into a Real Ministry

Smart Love

A Field Guide
for Single Adults

Nancy L. Van Pelt

Fleming H. Revell
A Division of Baker Book House
Grand Rapids, Michigan 49516

Published by Fleming H. Revell
a division of Baker Book House Company
P.O. Box 6287, Grand Rapids, MI 49516-6287

Printed in the United States of America

Library of Congress Cataloging-in-Publication Data

Van Pelt, Nancy L.
    Smart love : a field guide for single adults / Nancy L. Van Pelt.
        p. cm.
    ISBN 0-8007-5622-3 (trade paper)
    1. Dating (Social customs)—United States—Religious aspects—Christianity. 2. Man-woman relationships—United States—Religious aspects—Christianity. 3. Sex—United States—Religious aspects—Christianity. I. Title.
HQ801.V28 1997
646.7'7—dc21   96-52293

For current information about all releases from Baker Book House, visit our web site: http://www.bakerbooks.com/

Dedicated to
all single adults
who are in love,
will sometime fall in love,
or wish they were in love . . .
those like

Cathy	Bill
Karen	Richard
Laura	Douglas
Pam	George
Beth	Leroy
Linda	Rodney
Diane	Gene
Norma	Ken
Carol	Scott
Judy	Dan

Here's hoping you can experience how wonderful love can be when two lives and two hearts so intertwine that they desire above all else to share the fulfillment of a lifelong blessing of God's design—marriage.

There are four things that are too mysterious for me to understand:
  an eagle flying in the sky,
  a snake moving on a rock,
  a ship finding its way over the sea,
    and a man and a woman falling in love.

Proverbs 30:18–19 GNB

Contents

Before You Begin

S ome of you have been looking for love in all the wrong places. Some of you have fallen for all the wrong people. Others have failed at love more times than you care to count. Many singles feel much like Leo the cat.

Leo is a stately, all-white, furry cat who belongs to my friend Jean. Poor Leo never saw it coming. One day he lived in a peaceful household with Jean and her family. The next day he was bruised, staggering, hot, bothered, and definitely cross-eyed.

The problem began when Leo's owner checked on a load of clothes in the dryer. She opened the door of the dryer and found that half the load was still damp. So she sorted through the load and removed the dry items, carrying them to the next room to be folded. Then she returned to the laundry room to restart the dryer.

This is where the trouble began. No sooner had the dryer begun turning than she heard a loud and rhythmic thump . . . thump . . . thump . . . similar to the sound of tennis shoes being dried in a clothes dryer. She didn't recall tennis shoes being in the load of clothes. Then terror-stricken, she thought of Leo. She gasped, reached for the dryer door, and pulled it open. There was Leo—alive but stunned.

Poor Leo. He never knew what hit him. He lived through the trauma but was a bit dazed and seemed to stagger afterward. Jean never could get his fur to lie flat again. I asked

Jean how Leo was doing. "Well," she replied, "Leo doesn't purr much anymore. He just sits and stares."

It's easy to understand why.

Just as Leo was bruised, ruffled, and cross-eyed, so are many singles who have been through an unhappy relationship. They are still going around in circles—even though they are out of the dryer.

Maybe you are one who has had your share of dead-end relationships and disappointments. While trying not to give up on finding love, you are lonely and unfulfilled. You may live a busy life—own your own business and have a successful career, plenty of friends, and a full social schedule. Yet you know you're missing out by not having someone special with whom to share your life. Vague feelings of discontent haunt you as you attempt to concentrate on career, church, and other interests rather than on the empty hole in your heart. While successful in other areas of life, you've been unsuccessful in establishing a long-term relationship.

Others of you may be late bloomers. You've pursued an extensive education and taken time to establish a career. You possess self-worth and promise and have an unblemished future before you. But though reasonably good-looking and intelligent, you've never found that special someone.

Still others of you have fallen into sin more times than you care to count. One-night stands and promiscuity have become the name of the game. This book is for you too. If you'll give God the past and let Him bury it, this book can be your guide to the clean, healthy, happy future you've always wanted.

Whatever the circumstances, most of you have been drifting in and out of unsuccessful relationships, not realizing it is possible to have more control over future relationships than you have had in the past. It is possible to learn behaviors that will help move a relationship forward to commitment.

You may be floundering because you never learned how to manage romance. And that is what this book is all about. I have extensively researched this subject and measured it all against biblical standards. As I've taught courses on "romance management" over the years, I've realized the truth that romance can be managed much like a career or business. But just as some people have no educational, career, or business goals, many have little education and no goals concerning relationships. They aimlessly drift along, at the mercy of circumstances and other people.

If you are one of those who is at the mercy of circumstances, I hope you are ready for a change and that you will read this book with an open mind, incorporating what is needed into your present lifestyle. Remember, if what you have been doing in the past hasn't resulted in what you desired, then it is time to try a different approach. This book will show you how. What could be more satisfying? You can take control of your love life! You don't have to just wait around hoping something great will happen!

This book will help you do the following:

Stop drifting and take charge of your relationship
Educate yourself about what you want and need from the opposite sex
Avoid relationships with emotionally unhealthy persons
End dead-end relationships forever

I've observed that many people spend less time seriously considering what they want from a relationship than they spend on what clothes they will wear to work the next day. If you want to find someone to love you, with whom you can have a satisfying, nourishing relationship, you must have a plan of action.

Dating for an adult single is vastly different than for a teenager in high school. Addressed here will be the more sophisticated and complicated issues of love, dating, and sex for the mature single—the one who no longer has parents to answer to or the one who is trying to date and parent too. This book is for the person who is attempting to live a pure life in the midst of a sexual jungle, the one who is trying to find forgiveness for innumerable dating mistakes, the one who is reentering the dating arena after divorce or death of a spouse, and the one who wishes to follow God's principles.

Most of us have had very little instruction in how to choose a mate and yet we are expected to make a brilliant choice. Statistics indicate how often we are wrong. We desperately need to reevaluate mate-selection procedures! And this book is my attempt to make a difference, beginning with you. As a Certified Family Life Educator, I will explain how to establish healthy relationships *before problems develop.* Unlike a counselor who assists people with solutions after a problem occurs or the relationship breaks down, I will help you develop skills so that you can make better choices and be more successful in love than you have been in the past. My goal for this book is to help you make a wise choice in the person you marry.

The probability of your having a great marriage can be significantly increased if you adhere to carefully formulated principles. Those who count on luck and chance, passion and romance alone are those who are going to end up with disappointing marriages or in divorce court.

Most of us are acutely aware that divorce is responsible for much of the chaos and agony people are experiencing. But with guidance, your choice of a marriage partner can be made skillfully and wisely. The principles in this book comprise recent scientific research and durable biblical teaching. When you combine these two sources of wisdom, you will have a significantly better chance of making wise decisions about the person you marry.

Your choice of a marriage partner is one of the most important decisions you'll ever make. If you choose wisely, your life will be satisfying and fulfilling. If you make a serious mistake and your marriage fails, it will cause you and your children, and all the generations to follow, immeasurable pain.

The theme of this book is prevention—preventing unhealthy relationships and the heartache that follows. I advocate taking time for relationships to develop. The best way to prevent getting involved in an unhealthy relationship and the tragedy that follows is to slow down. Slowing down romantic relationships allows time to carefully analyze your emotional health and the emotional readiness of your dating partner and provides the opportunity for hidden difficulties to appear.

I have a real problem with people jumping into relationships. I have seen too much pain. It has become a basic tenet of my seminars, writing, and counsel, and it is a well-researched fact that healthy relationships develop over time. The following letter illustrates a scenario I see far too frequently:

Dear Nancy,

I am forty-four years old and in love with a wonderful man I met two months ago. He is so kind and treats me better than I've ever been treated in my life. We truly love each other and plan to be married in five months.

We've been sleeping together and I feel really guilty about this. I told Jim how I felt and he doesn't want to hurt me in any way. So sometimes we sleep together in the same bed but refrain from having sex. How do you see this?

Please forgive me for being so blunt with you, but I sometimes relieve his sexual drives through oral sex. Is this okay for a couple who is going to get married in five months?

I really love this man and know he loves me. He isn't the same religion I am but he is a Christian and we both want to obey God. My divorce will be final in five months and I know I can finally be free of my past. My last husband sexually abused our daughter and physically abused me. I am so happy I found Jim and want to marry him just as soon as possible. I don't want to miss one month of happiness I know he will bring into my life. I deserve it, since I've had such a miserable past. Jim will make my life wonderful!

Signed: Guilty in Wisconsin

"Guilty in Wisconsin" is breaking every rule of good sense for wise mate selection. To name a few:

13

- The decision to marry has been made too quickly.
- She seeks marriage as an answer to a miserable past.
- She has unrealistic expectations for future happiness.
- There has been insufficient time to observe any personality or behavioral problems in Jim.
- There is sexual involvement, which clouds the emotional development of the relationship.
- They are dating prior to the closure of her previous marriage.
- She has emotional trauma due to physical abuse.

Like "Guilty in Wisconsin," most unmarried people look to marriage to solve past problems and make them happy. They assume a quick trip to the altar will ensure happiness. Often the greater their problems, the faster they rush. But weddings do not automatically change anyone nor do they ensure happiness. Feelings of romantic excitement greatly cloud the realities involved in a long-term marriage and the sacrifices a couple must make for the relationship to work. And it certainly is not possible to survive if the relationship is rushed or the two people have not dealt with their own brokenness.

My prayer is that God will use the principles here to help you learn, easier and sooner than others, how to build and maintain successful dating relationships that may eventually lead to a harmonious and mutually satisfying marriage.

We serve a magnificent God. Regardless of your past, God can salvage your life. I can't promise that as a result of reading this book you will find the perfect partner and live happily ever after. But I know that we serve a God who is masterful in turning ashes into gold. My prayer is that His Spirit will speak to you on every page regarding His will for your life.

Part 1
Self-Worth

1

Prerequisite for Love

Nat, a thirty-six-year-old telephone executive from New Orleans, desperately wants to meet a woman he can fall in love with. But every time he thinks about dating someone new his mind plays reruns of failed romances. When he met Connie, a friendly physician's assistant, it was all he could do to ask her out. He knew the date would be disastrous and sure enough it was. In spite of the fact that he was attracted to her and she appeared to like him, he was so self-conscious, he was miserable. When he did talk, he said the wrong things. He was so uptight that he had no sense of humor. Nat's lack of self-worth had already cost him several relationships and it cost him one more.

Jeannie has had a couple of dates with a man she is beginning to like. Since he said he would call this evening, she waits by the phone. When he finally calls, he tells her that he's not been totally honest with her. He likes her but he's in a relationship with another woman that he cannot get out of at present. Jeannie is devastated. After hanging up, she cries uncontrollably, in spite of attempts to convince herself she'll get over it. She feels miserable and spends the next month berating herself. "Every relationship I've ever had ends up like this," she whimpers over and over. "I knew it wouldn't last. He really didn't care for me at all. None of my dates ever gets to the serious stage. Something is really wrong with me."

To all the Nats and Jeannies of the world, if you don't change how you think and feel about yourself, you'll end up dating and marrying the wrong kind of person. The poor image of self you harbor will attract someone who will try to control, parent, or fix you. Because you don't like yourself, you may allow someone to abuse you physically or emotionally.

To establish an emotionally healthy relationship, a person needs a positive self-image. Unless you like yourself, you are neither capable of making intelligent decisions about love nor ready to form a romantic relationship with another person.

The concept we have of self is the basis from which we act and react. It determines how we choose our values, select our goals, and formulate our belief system. Our response to life events is shaped to a large extent by who and what we think about self. Remember: Self-image is not what you actually are. Ninety percent of self-image revolves around what you think others think of you. In effect, we allow others to determine our self-image!

Sometimes our perception of what others think is false. It is possible to be loved by parents, children, and friends and not love oneself. One can be admired by work associates and still feel worthless because of other experiences that have had a negative impact on self-image. Honors and awards can be won by those who feel useless because self-esteem comes from within. Success in the eyes of the world does not spell success inside.

The self-concept, then, is formed from a combination of all past experiences and relationships, our successes and failures, and what we think others think about us.

Many definitions of self-esteem have been given, but Nathaniel Branden, Ph.D., a pioneer in the field of understanding self-esteem, gives the most complete one. "Self-esteem is the experience of being competent to cope with the basic challenges of life and of being worthy of happiness." "Self-respect," according to Dr. Branden, "is confidence in our right to be happy; confidence that achievement, success, friendship, respect, love, and fulfillment are appropriate to us."[1]

When you feel like this about yourself, you will be able to establish healthy love relationships, earn a living, take independent care of yourself, bounce back from pain and adversity, and pursue and achieve successful life goals.

Self-worth is the center of emotional and mental health. If you genuinely know and respect yourself, you have laid a solid foundation that equips you to handle the daily challenges of life. When you possess a poor self-image and shaky self-confidence, you cannot maintain control of your life.

No relationship can be healthier than the two persons involved. A critical question for two people to answer before considering a lifelong partnership is: How solid is our individual self-worth? If either one has a fragile or poor sense of self, the couple will be susceptible to endless emotional trauma. It takes energy and maturity to manage the inner life. It is emotional and mental stability that produces marital strength and happiness. When one or both aren't healthy there is the probability that their relationship will be damaged and eventually fall apart.

All the Negative Garbage

Feelings of worth are learned, not inherited. Initially feelings of worth are formed during childhood. When parents love and value a child and such feelings are conveyed in a positive manner over a period of time, the child concludes he is special. The opposite can also be true. When a child is

19

repeatedly ridiculed, he begins to accept this evaluation as valid. A lack of affirmation from parents who are too busy or ignorant to provide it can be just as devastating. The effects last a lifetime. Those with a poor self-image resulting from childhood trauma must first heal those early wounds before they can progress to healthy adult relationships.

Those from dysfunctional homes—alcoholic parents, physically and/or emotionally abusive parents, or parents who neglected them—begin to believe the message that they are no good. Often such children begin to believe that if they had been good enough, their parents wouldn't have gotten drunk and wouldn't have beaten or neglected them. If they had been good enough, their parents would have loved, nurtured, and affirmed them.

Society also plays a part in promoting feelings of inferiority. Prizes are offered to winners, honors given to the intelligent, and awards presented to the beautiful and popular. Commercials tell us that to be accepted we must use certain products, wear certain clothes, and look a certain way. A person may feel inferior because he was forced to wear hand-me-downs, has a large nose, is a member of a minority race or religion, or has a physical handicap.

> *In 1856, Eliza Emily Donnithorne of Sydney, Australia, was supposed to be married, but her husband-to-be never showed up. Heartbroken, she never left her house for thirty years. She even locked the room where the wedding celebration was supposed to be held, leaving the cake and decorations in place to rot.*
>
> *It is believed that her tragedy gave Charles Dickens the idea for his famous Miss Havisham character in his novel* Great Expectations.
>
> The Wrong Stuff

A survey by *Psychology Today* on body image showed that more than 60 percent of both sexes feel their looks are a liability to them. Those who were teased about their appearance as children are much more likely to carry the residual effects into adulthood than those who did not like their appearance but were not teased about it.

Psychology Today's survey, as well as numerous other studies, confirms that self-worth is deeply affected by appearance. While there are exceptions, generally speaking, the higher you rate your looks, the higher your self-worth. The less satisfied you are with your personal appearance, the lower your feelings of worth.

The Far-Reaching Consequences of a Poor Self-Concept

The consequences of a poor self-concept are far-reaching. Not only does a poor self-concept warp the person's feelings about himself, but it also reaches out and affects everyone with whom the individual interacts—including all romantic interests.

A poor self-concept limits your capacity to love and accept others. It's a simple fact. You cannot love someone else unless you first have a healthy self-like. You can genuinely love and receive love from others in direct proportion to how you feel about yourself. If you cannot like yourself, then you cannot like others. If you do not feel secure and worthwhile at the very core of your being, you cannot like or respect others.

A poor self-concept influences your choice of dating partners. The person who lacks self-respect often picks a partner who will devalue, criticize, or put him down. Why? Because this treatment re-creates feelings to which he has become accustomed. He feels comfortable with it.

A poor self-concept influences the future of your children. Parents pass poor self-concept on to their children. You may think you hide it so well that no one will ever find out. But your children are able to see in your attitudes toward yourself and life that you do not respect yourself, and they will not respect you either. Unconsciously they pick up the same tendencies toward poor self-concept. It is difficult for a person with a poor self-concept to pass on to his children a healthy self-image unless someone or something else is able to compensate.

A poor self-concept affects your sex life. Sex is commonly used to boost a weak self-image. An insecure male might try to prove to himself and others how great he is by having sex. An insecure female might try to hold on to a man through sex, thereby making herself feel desirable and secure in the relationship. Both are using sex to prove they have value and worth.

Such strategies backfire. Within marriage sex includes love, trust, security, and freedom. Within a permanent commitment there is no need to prove anything or use the other as an ego booster or a security blanket. God provided a perfect arrangement, but people are still trying to sidestep His plan.

A poor self-concept may cause you to tolerate abuse. Fran, a thirty-three-year-old receptionist, said she began self-destructive behavior early. By age thirteen she was having sex regularly with a boyfriend so she wouldn't lose him. By fourteen she was pregnant and had her first abortion. By seventeen she was on a binge of sleeping with anyone. By her own admission she hated herself. "I was attracted to men who would emotionally abuse me, physically use me, and eventually reject and abandon me. I would put up with anything. My experience with men taught me that I'm not worth much. I subconsciously set myself up, time after time, by becoming involved with men who would treat me this way."

Those with poor self-concept put up with abuse and other destructive behaviors because they think they don't deserve better. They actually believe they are worthless and look for and feel comfortable in love relationships where this idea is confirmed. Because of their low opinion of themselves and the tendency to repeat self-destructive behaviors, they will date anyone who shows an interest.

A poor self-concept diverts attention to false goals. If you truly feel you are worthless, you may try to gain acceptance by pursuing goals that will bring you the approval of others. For instance, some people strive for unattainable perfection, buy expensive clothing, drive foreign cars, and live in elegantly furnished homes in an effort to cover up feelings of inadequacy. Accumulating material possessions has diverted their attention from more important goals. As a result, their search for self-acceptance goes on and on, because things cannot boost up an unstable self-concept.

A poor self-concept hinders spiritual growth. We all have trouble from time to time with trusting God, but the person with low self-worth will feel even more troubled about his inability to trust God. And this person will have difficulty having faith in God. This inability to trust God can often be traced to a deep rejection of self. One woman reasoned this way: "God created everything, didn't He? He is supposed to be wise and everlastingly loving. If what I see in the mirror is an example of His creation and His love, then I'm not interested in that kind of God."

Such feelings are usually not conscious. More often than not they are unconscious murmurings but they have a strong negative impact on one's relationship with God.

Cover-ups We Wear to Mask Our Pain

Art Buchwald once said, "Humor is a mask. It is a way of hiding emotion." Yes, humor is a mask comedians often use to cope with the pain and hurt from their past. And just as they hide behind humor, so do others hide behind masks and reactions to cover pain. Let's look at several of these.

Withdrawal. Mary has surmised from past experience she is inferior and cannot attract a man. Completely surrendered to this evaluation she concludes she is worthless and will never marry. In order to protect herself from further rejection, she withdraws from social situations into a shell of silence and loneliness. As Mary journeys through life, she carefully protects herself from meeting men and from any situations that involve emotional risk. Never will she initiate a conversation, speak up in a group, or defend her ideas. In so doing Mary has become less capable of developing and maintaining a love relationship. Without realizing it, her deductions about herself have closed the door on love.

Comparison. People who feel inferior are always comparing themselves to others and coming up short. John was attracted to Becky, who invited him to go to a party with her. John went but had a miserable time as he felt the other men there had better jobs, were better looking, or were better dressed than he. Even though John desperately wanted to see Becky again, he never called because he felt so inferior. Becky became engaged to one of John's best friends. At dinner one evening when discussing old times, Becky told John how much she had wanted to see him again after that party! John lost to another guy because he compared himself to the competition and accepted defeat! Every time you compare yourself to someone else, you will come out second best. When you feel second best, you will act second best.

Jealousy. Jealousy is a reaction that is prompted by fear—the fear of losing someone who means a lot to us. Yet the tighter we cling, the more ground we lose. Fear and possessiveness breed contempt and actually drive others from us. Feelings of insecurity and lack of personal identity invite rejection and cause others to feel stifled. Emotionally healthy persons may feel slightly jealous from time to time but are not consumed by unreasoning and continual bouts of jealousy.

Criticism. Barb is always bragging about her home, pool, car, clothes, and job while criticizing what others have. Attempting to make herself look better, she tries to make others appear worse. Criticism and put-downs drive people away entirely or make any friendships very unsatisfactory.

Fear of intimacy. It has already been established that you cannot love others until you first have a healthy self-like. If you don't like yourself you will become fearful when someone attempts to get to know you. More than anything you want friends but you fear they will reject you once they know the real you. So you keep people at a distance, never allowing them close enough to get to know you.

> *In 1977, an extremely small, skinny Italian man developed an attraction for large English women. While dancing with an English woman, however, he suddenly fainted. Doctors discovered that he had been wearing seventeen wool sweaters to make himself look heftier.*
>
> The Incomplete Book of Failures

The Effect of Self-Image on Relationships

When your self-image is positive, you tend to seek relationships that will reinforce positive feelings. The opposite is also true. When you are consumed by negative feelings about self, you will seek relationships that confirm worthlessness. When you feel like a nobody inside, when fearful and easily depressed, you will be easily swayed by the attentions of anyone who woos or flatters you, regardless of who it is. When you lack the ability to validate your own worth, you tend to follow others around like a puppy, dependent on them for attaining a sense of significance.

Some people are so lacking in self-worth and are so afraid of being abandoned, they will cling in desperation to any relationship, even one that brings pain. It doesn't have to be this way. To avoid getting into a destructive relationship, you must be ruthlessly honest about your own brokenness. If you are carrying hurt and pain from the past, have unfinished business with parents or previous relationships, or have a self-image so poor you will permit abuse, you need healing before you begin dating. Dating is beyond your capabilities for now. Back off from emotional involvements. If you have brokenness in your life, admit it now and seek help. Al Anon and other twelve-step programs and private professional counseling can give you the help you need

> *Some companies are willing to insure the strangest things . . . even love relationships. If the love relationship crumbles, the policyholder collects insurance money.*
>
> The Wrong Stuff

before you endanger your future as well as someone else's.

Building self-esteem, learning to feel entitled to happiness, and expecting good things to come your way are important elements in being ready for romance. Some people appear naturally to have a healthy self-image. Others struggle to find it. Still others must spend long hours in therapy before they can achieve it.

You can often tell by the way a person looks and acts that he does not like himself. Picture Charlie Brown from the *Peanuts* series. The slump of his shoulders, hands in his pockets, and down-turned mouth all tell a story without the caption: "Nobody cares if I live or die."

A weak self-image will bind and keep you from achieving what you really want. It will force you to stick with the safety of the known and familiar rather than challenging you to achieve new and worthwhile goals. If your aspirations are low, you won't achieve much. But the higher your self-esteem the higher your aspirations will be for achieving success—emotionally, financially, intellectually, spiritually, and romantically.

The poorer your self-image the greater the urge to prove something and to impress others. The better your self-image the easier it is to be yourself without having to put on airs. Low self-concept will cause defensive and inappropriate communication patterns to dominate due to unclear goals and a concern to protect a weak sense of being. The stronger the self-esteem the more open, honest, and clear your communication patterns will be because you have thought through your values, goals, and beliefs and have confidence in them.

If you hope to achieve a healthy, happy relationship with a member of the opposite sex, this factor of self-esteem is the most important. _The greatest barriers to successful romance are feelings of worthlessness, inadequacy, and failure._ The first relationship in which you must achieve success is a love relationship with yourself. You must first feel that you are worthy and lovable. Then you are more likely to be able to negotiate loving relationships with others. Only when you can first love yourself will you be able to accept love from others.

Part of loving self is being happy with how you look. This has a lot to do with how you present yourself to the opposite sex. And how you present yourself has a sharp impact on how successful you are in attracting dates. If you feel you are not physically attractive, you may fear to approach an attractive person who catches your attention.

How you feel about yourself and how you present yourself also determine what kind of person you are likely to attract. It is hardly surprising then that those with a slovenly appearance rate themselves as dissatisfied with their opposite-sex relationships.

When evaluating your self-esteem you must look at what relationships you presently have that are validating your worth and which are detrimental to your feelings of worth. If a relationship is destructive and negative, you must choose to end the relationship or to change it so that the impact of it is positive. It takes effort to change old patterns of interaction and create new ones to improve relationships, but if you sincerely want to feel better about yourself, you need to invest in relationships that will contribute positively to your self-esteem.

Divorce—A Blow to Self-Esteem

Maybe you have been through a divorce. There is probably no time in a person's life when he feels so worthless as when a marriage ends. Marriage is a very personal part of a person's existence and when it fails, the people involved feel like failures.

Even if you are the one who initiated the divorce, or were not at fault, or did not desire the divorce, or were the "innocent party," or tried your best to keep the marriage intact, you will not escape the emotional crisis that accompanies divorce.

When you enter a love relationship, you receive much validation from the other person. When a marriage ends, there has already been massive destructive impact on each partner's self-concept. For some people, their self-concept has suffered so much they can't even take the necessary steps to end the marriage. This is often the case with battered women.

To the same degree that falling in love is exciting, falling out of love is painful. The devastating hurt comes from the deep sense of rejection. The period of a divorce is likely to be when self-concept reaches an all-time low.

One positive side effect of this experience is that it can also cause you to take a closer look at yourself than you ever did before. It could be a powerful force in motivating you to make some much needed changes in your life and your perception of self.

Self-esteem is fragile. It can be intact one minute and gone the next. We may endure two or three setbacks, but when another one comes along, it brings on a crisis of confidence. The worth we ascribe to ourselves, especially in romantic relationships, is so vulnerable that even tough people barely make it at times. The one who lacks self-respect is going to find it very difficult to have good relationships with the opposite sex.

Positive Self-Image

Self-worth should be an honest appraisal of self. "Do not think of yourself more highly than you ought, but rather think of yourself with sober judgment" (Rom. 12:3). We should not rate ourselves too highly; neither should we underestimate our value. Some people try to make low self-image a virtue by identifying it with humility as opposed to arrogance and pride—their definition of high self-esteem. But high self-esteem is not arrogance. When we have high self-esteem, we feel equal to, not better than others—adequate to cope with the responsibilities of life.

We make no false claims. Rather, we accept our weak areas as well as our strengths and feel we deserve the respect of others. We have learned to build on strengths and compensate for weaknesses. We have learned to live with the limitations we have been unable to change. From time to time we fail but we are able to pick up the pieces and move ahead. We try to be sincere and open and we consider that we are worthwhile.

Healthy self-respect frees us to pay attention to others. We can then be as tolerant of the weaknesses of others as we are of our own. We can appreciate the differences of others instead of resenting, fearing, or ridiculing them. We realize that this differentness makes each human being unique. Healthy self-respect also frees us spiritually, for we can more fully appreciate God's acceptance of us as we are and the potential for good within us.

Dr. Nathaniel Branden believes there are six key virtues on which self-esteem depends: living consciously, self-acceptance, self-responsibility, self-assertiveness, living purposefully, and personal integrity.[2]

- *To live consciously* is to understand who and what you are. The choices you make day by day determine your values, goals, and beliefs.
- *To be self-accepting* means that you recognize your imperfections and mistakes as well as your strengths. You are able to put failures behind you and build on strengths to compensate for the weaknesses. What cannot be changed is accepted.
- *To be self-responsible* is to recognize that your future happiness, success, or failure is determined by the choices you make through your words, actions, and emotions and that no one else is responsible for making you happy.
- *To be self-assertive* is being willing to stand and speak for your convictions, values, and feelings as well as learning appropriate ways to express your wants and needs.
- *To live purposefully* is to think through meaningful life goals, to choose actions that lead toward those goals, and to check periodically to see if you are moving toward your chosen goals.
- *To live with integrity* is to choose principles and values that govern your life and living, through word and deed, according to those principles.

Think what it would mean to live by these virtues! Think what it would mean to establish a lifelong relationship with a person who lived by them! Men and women with high self-esteem are drawn to each other. Likewise, people with low self-esteem are also drawn to each other and form destructive relationships. Possessing an adequate measure of each of these six virtues, then, is the most important element in establishing a healthy romantic relationship.

When You Are Emotionally Healthy but Your Partner Isn't

If after careful evaluation you recognize that your self-worth is solid but your dating partner's is low, what should you do? *Slow down.* The person who is unhappy with himself before marriage will not be happy after marriage. Marriage is relatively easy when both partners feel good about self. The person with positive feelings of worth will be able to freely give love, compassion, and forgiveness and will be cooperative and will accept responsibility. This person has confidence in his own abilities and is free to appreciate the worth of others and accept others as they are. Problems may arise, disappointments mount, fatigue press hard, but somehow the high self-esteem person manages.

The person with a poor self-image, however, has difficulty solving problems constructively because this person is buried in myriad self-defeating patterns. Desperation overwhelms him as problems surface. Since this person possesses neither the coping mechanism to resolve his problems nor the ability to put new skills to work, he will sink deeper into self-defeating patterns. Obviously this affects all relationships. The person with a poor self-image is often unhappy and will likely sink into terrible states of depression and indifference or lash out at his partner with blame for the hurt and pain.

Rather than risking your future happiness by marrying a person with a poor self-concept, why not wait for your dating partner to get the help that is needed prior to marriage? Why risk your entire future hoping he will change?

Dr. Stanley S. Heller, a distinguished psychiatrist who was selected by *New York* magazine as one of the top New

York City psychiatrists, has said, "The most important quality in any marriage is the emotional health of each person." You can avoid a lifetime of heartache and gain a lifetime of happiness by being sure that you and your partner are healthy. If the one you love refuses to get the necessary help to correct self-esteem problems, you must move on to someone who is healthy, a person who is capable of nourishing a relationship even when the inevitable stress occurs.

It is more difficult than ever to find an emotionally healthy partner because a record number of people are growing up in dysfunctional homes—families that have been ravaged by divorce, alcoholism, drug abuse, and emotional, sexual, or physical abuse. Though few know it, such persons carry devastating wounds. Their personal pain drives them to search for someone who can heal their pain, soothe their wounds, and put together all the broken pieces of their lives. When you enter the dating arena, carefully evaluate each dating partner. Look beneath surface issues. Rush into nothing. Take your time and wait for hidden difficulties to erupt.

If you ever hope to have a happy love relationship that will last a lifetime, no factor is more important than self-esteem—in you and in your partner. There is no greater barrier to romantic success than deep-seated feelings that you are unlovable. The first love affair you must negotiate successfully is a love affair with yourself. Only then will you be ready for romance. Only then will you be fully able to love another person and allow the other person to love you. Without the knowledge that you are lovable, the other person's love will never be quite real or convincing to you. In many insidious ways, you will unknowingly attempt to undermine it.

The bottom line in romance is that if you possess high self-worth, you will more likely feel like a million dollars. If you feel like a million dollars, you are more likely to think and act like a million dollars. If you think and act like a million dollars, you are more likely to attract those who also feel, think, and act like a million dollars.

As Oscar Wilde once said, "To love oneself is the beginning of a life-long romance."

2

Improving Your Self-Image

You Can Learn to Like Yourself and Win at Love

Recognizing a lack of self-esteem in yourself or someone else is one thing. Struggling to overcome its crippling effects is another. If you have been condemning yourself because of past failures, embarrassments, and rejections, it is time to free yourself. The sooner you decide to make friends with yourself, the sooner you will be ready to build a healthy relationship with someone else.

There are no easy solutions for long-term, deep-seated problems of inferiority, but if you wish to change those negative feelings about yourself, change is possible! Since the self-concept is learned from past life experiences, it can be unlearned. You simply replace negative feelings about yourself with positive ones. The older you are and the longer you have lived with a negative evaluation, the more difficult it will be. But it can be done! You don't have to stay the way you are today.

Remember, though, leaving behind a lifetime of self-hate is a process. It won't happen all at once. You can't undo years of self-hate in one step. You can, however, begin now to make small steps to free yourself of the past.

If your self-concept is really low, how much improvement can you expect to make in your feelings about yourself? The answer lies in how much effort you are willing to put into it. If you are willing to make superficial changes in insignificant matters, then the change will be minimal. For example, rather than stacking the dishes all week, you decide to wash them after each meal. Since little emotional energy is needed to make this change, it is easily accomplished. However, if you have had forty-two years of thinking negatively about yourself and you wish to begin thinking positively, it will take a great deal of effort and energy. The greater the change desired, the more investment it requires.

First, you need a desire to change. People with low self-esteem often lack the desire to change their attitudes and behavior patterns. They lack the ambition and drive to overcome previously ingrained tendencies. The truth is you can't do it alone. But when you give your desire over to the Lord, he can accomplish the change in you. Success is possible through him.

You must realize that when you decide to improve your self-concept, it will affect all your relationships and every aspect of your life—your work, your spiritual life, how you parent your children, as well as the kind of romantic relationship you will build. Enormous changes will take place in your personality and your life.

Now let's combine your desire to change and Christ's power with some practical suggestions. Then get ready to enjoy the benefits:

Let Go of the Past

We tend to respond and react to others on the basis of unresolved issues and conflicts from the past. Why continue to wallop yourself with the same old hurts? Why get stuck in a rut with a painful past? Forgiveness is the key that sets you free—forgiveness of self and others. Forgive to the point you will no longer allow what formerly happened to torment you. Forgiveness simply says: "I was deeply hurt by what happened. But I no longer resent you. I give all my hateful feelings to God. I can now accept and love you even if you cannot love and accept me." Only when you redirect negative memories to positive ones are you really free to move forward and love yourself as well as others.

Holding on to the past means you can't progress with the future. This will keep you spinning in an endless cycle of self-depreciation. It will press you down, bind, and defeat you. So letting go is actually a beginning.

Inventory Your Strengths

We rarely take time for a balanced self-appraisal. Most of us focus on our weak areas—all the things we can't do, our limitations. Instead of focusing on what we can't do, we need to focus on the positive—what we *can* do.

Use the chart below to list your strengths.

Achievements

Appearance

Personality

Talents & Skills

Character & Spiritual Abilities

In each category list at least three strengths. Under "Achievements" think of raises, promotions, awards, or other personal successes. Go back in time if need be. Under "Appearance" list things like physically fit, attractive, clear skin, bright eyes. Under "Personality" include good sense of humor, calm nature, friendly, pleasant disposition. Under "Talents & Skills": What natural gifts and aptitudes do you possess? Include musical or artistic ability, cooking, organizing, and scholastic and athletic abilities. Under "Character & Spiritual Abilities" list such things as high standards, integrity, honesty, and values. Christian service and being a prayer warrior would be spiritual abilities.

As you contemplate your personal attributes in each category remember that "we are God's workmanship, created in Christ Jesus to do good works, which God prepared in advance for us to do" (Eph. 2:10). You are not boasting but simply recognizing and praising God for the good work He has begun in you. This list of positive traits should help you recognize that you have tremendous potential and many talents to work with.

Rebuild Your Thought Patterns

A psychologist counseled many women over the age of thirty who appeared to harbor feelings of hopelessness regarding their marriageability. Most had reached the stage of "I guess I'll never get married." These women were bright, attractive, and successful women who had a lot to offer the right man. Yet they felt doomed to spend their lives alone. Although these women were all different from one another, they all shared one thing in common: negative thinking and behavior that sabotaged their relationships. The psychologist wondered if their repeated negative thinking patterns could be the reason why they were unable to find lasting love. After an in-depth examination of thousands of men and women through videotapes, personality profiles, and individual interviews, it was clear: Women over thirty who wanted to be married and weren't showed exactly the same negative thought patterns the psychologist's clients had demonstrated. Even more important, the women who found someone, fell in love, and got married showed the exact opposite patterns of thinking and behavior. They followed "success patterns" from the beginning.[1] Rebuilding thought patterns and imagining yourself to be successful really work!

> *Having problems may not be so bad. We have a special place for folks who have none—it's called a cemetery.*
>
> Frank A. Clark

Once negative thoughts take hold, they can be hard to change. We actually look for proof for what we already think about ourselves. So if you think others don't like you, you will actually look for things that seem to prove this.

Some typical examples of negative self-talk might sound like this:

- I'm afraid to meet someone new.
- I'm not good-looking.
- I'm not a good conversationalist.
- I feel awkward when out socially.
- All the good men/women are taken.
- I never meet anyone interesting.
- I'm afraid to love because I might get hurt.
- All my relationships end in disaster.
- My mother always said no one would marry me.

The good news is it is possible to get a new script. Negative thought patterns can be controlled. The first step is awareness of negative patterns. Then begin catching negative thoughts as they come into your mind and replace them with positive self-talk. Each of the previous negative statements can be rephrased positively:

- I have a friendly personality that attracts others to me.
- I am an attractive person who possesses many positive traits.
- I will smile at people and be friendly.
- I am a happy person who attracts people.
- I look forward to loving someone who will love me in return.
- I look forward to meeting someone soon who will be interested in me.
- I'm looking forward to a great romance and am preparing for it by being positive.
- I am preparing myself now for a great romance that will last a lifetime.
- I choose to ignore negative messages from the past and will focus on positive hope for the future, which includes being ready for a healthy love relationship.

Repetition is the key to changing negative thinking patterns to positive ones. Your affirmations need to be repeated twenty to thirty times a day or more. Hint: Repeat your affirmations aloud while looking into a mirror. Smile at yourself (If you find that difficult to do, wink at yourself. I guarantee you will smile!) and then repeat the affirmations aloud. According to behavioral experts it takes twenty-one to forty-five days of repetition to change a habit. If you consistently work at rebuilding your thought patterns, you'll feel better about you in twenty-one to forty-five days! Don't expect miracles overnight. Give yourself time to change. Be kind to yourself while waiting for old attitudes to disappear.

Develop Admirable Qualities

By developing admirable skills, abilities, or personality and character traits, you can boost your self-esteem. If you are a poor conversationalist, terribly self-conscious, ill at ease and feel you can never think of the right thing to say, do something about it. Attend a Dale Carnegie seminar, join Toastmasters, take a night school personality course, or read a book about the art of conversation. If you are plain in appearance, learn about posture, attractive hair-styles, social graces, and dressing for success and then make some changes. In other words, study and then begin to prac-tice what you have learned. Try out your "new self" on a close circle of friends, gradually transferring your newly acquired skills to new contacts. The world's more charm-ing people are not necessarily beautiful. If you can't make the grade as "most popular," don't weep over it. Instead learn racquetball, write short stories, or attend a class in French cooking. Do your best to become interesting and well rounded.

Develop the attitude that you are open to new experiences rather than remaining in some secure rut you have created for yourself. And concentrate on the strengths you listed earlier. Work to improve on them.

Never Compare Yourself with Others

The biggest single cause of a poor self-concept is com-paring self to others. We tend to judge ourselves and mea-sure ourselves not by our own standard but against some-one else's standard. When we do this, we will always come out second best. The end result of such reasoning is that we believe we are not worthy of happiness or success, that it would be out of place for us to use our own abilities or tal-ents because they aren't as good as what others have.

You do not have to look or act like anyone else. The truth is, you are not inferior; you are not superior. You are sim-ply you, equal to others and a unique individual. So stop comparing yourself with others. Let Christ be the only stan-dard you try to emulate.

Give of Yourself to Others

Our own needs and problems seem less overwhelming when we help others with their problems. There is less time to wallow in self-pity when actively seeking a solution to someone else's problems. For everyone who feels rejected, unloved, and unworthy, there is someone else who is worse off.

One study showed that when people are helping others, they experience relief from stress-related headaches and other aches and pains. This happens only when the giver helps voluntarily, because she wants to. If forced to help, for whatever reason, there was little benefit to the giver. The giver also had to become intimately involved, having close personal contact, with those being helped.

If you want to feel better both physically and mentally, bake something for a friend, surprise an elderly person with a small gift, visit the sick, sign up for volunteer work with an agency that needs help, give someone a ride, or listen to a friend with a problem. The world is crammed with lonely, discouraged people who need you to empathize with them. While you are doing all this, your own sense of inadequacy won't seem so acute. The best medicine for self-pity is to give of yourself to others.

Ask God to Make Something Beautiful out of Your Life

If you have had negative attitudes about yourself—resentment because of your appearance, your lack of talent, your singleness, or anything else, ask God to forgive you. Ask God to forgive

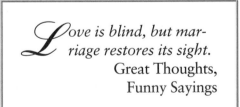

Love is blind, but marriage restores its sight.
Great Thoughts,
Funny Sayings

any bitterness you have had toward His creation—you.

Then thank God for creating you just the way you are. This will not be an easy step. You may feel you cannot thank God for creating you the way you are when you hate the way you are. You may think this makes you a hypocrite, that you can't thank God when you don't feel thankful. But you can do it even if you don't feel like it. Giving thanks is an act of the will. *Feeling* thankful is an emotion. Do not let your emotions control you. You can give thanks even though you don't feel like it. Set your will in the right direction, and your emotions will follow.

When you know that God accepts and loves you just the way you are, you don't have to feel as though you must change yourself. Your self-worth should not be programmed by others but rooted and grounded in the value God places on you. The only things God dislikes are things that would destroy you. He is interested only in helping you leave destructive attitudes and behaviors behind.

You are complete in Christ. You are accepted by Him, the King of the universe! When you know this, it frees you to be the you you've always wanted to be! God provides you with a fresh beginning if you are willing to obey His Word.

If you take God at His Word, believing that you are loved and worthwhile, then you have a solid base from which to operate. You will have a firm center to your life. You will be free to put the same kind of love and respect you have for yourself to work in your love relationships. Remember, you can never experience a true love relationship unless you first take care of any self-acceptance problems within you. Not only does God count you as acceptable, but He stands ready to work miracles in you, to change your worst failures and memories into successes—just as He did for Marjorie.

For years Marjorie had been burdened by broken self-esteem, seeing herself as unlovely, ungainly, untalented, un-intelligent, un-everything that makes people feel valuable and worthwhile as human beings. Over the years her self-hatred grew to a point where in desperation she turned to a Christian psychologist for help. He "walked" her back through her memories to a painful incident from her childhood.

Many years earlier, Marjorie had been caught in some minor act of misbehavior in her third-grade class. Her teacher—a harsh, vindictive disciplinarian—called Marjorie forward and stood her before the class. "Children," said the teacher, "I want each of you to come to the blackboard and write anything you dislike about this bad girl."

The next few minutes were a nightmare for Marjorie as, one by one, each child went forward and chalked hurtful statements about her in letters several inches tall. "Marjorie is ugly," wrote one. "Marjorie is fat," wrote another. "Marjorie is a slob." "Marjorie has no friends." "Marjorie is stupid." Standing before the class, Marjorie wished she could sink right through the floor and out of sight. It went on and on until all twenty-five classmates had filled the blackboard with hate and ugliness.

"Marjorie," said a kind voice. Gradually, Marjorie realized she was no longer back in school. She was in the present, in the psychologist's office, and the voice she had heard was his. Tears flooded her face, and sobs racked her body.

"Marjorie," the psychologist repeated when the tears subsided, "I want you to picture the classroom again—but there's a difference this time. There's a twenty-sixth student in the classroom with you, and his name is Jesus. Now imagine the scene with me: Jesus gets up from His desk and He walks past the teacher, ignoring the chalk she holds out to him. Instead of writing on the blackboard, He is erasing, erasing, erasing. Do you see it, Marjorie? The slate is clean now."

"Yes," she said. "Yes, I see it."

Now Jesus takes up the chalk and begins to write. "Marjorie is a beautiful child of God." "Marjorie is forgiven." "Marjorie will live forever."

For the first time in many years Marjorie began to feel valuable and loved. It was a giant first step along the path away from the crippling pain of mistreatment and toward wholeness.[2]

God did it for Marjorie. He can do it for you. Ask God to take over in your life. God will take care of whatever has been holding you back from becoming the person you ought to be. God wants to uncover your worth, but you must give Him permission to prepare the way for this adventure. Give Him a try.

Part 2
The Dating Game

3

How the Thirty-to-Sixty-Something Crowd Plays the Game

M any singles hate dating. In the movie *Hannah and Her Sisters,* Woody Allen ends a date with Dianne Wiest by comparing the evening to the Nuremberg Trial. That's how a lot of singles feel in midlife when they are part of the dating scene. They've had a lot of relationships that haven't worked. Yet they feel they can't turn down a date because time is running out and this person might just be the *one.*

Dating can be disappointing and frustrating once "young adult" years are behind you. But it doesn't have to be. There is potential for romance, closeness, excitement, personal growth, and great fun for the older single in the delightful ritual called "dating."

No one has all the answers anymore. Gone are the days of strict rules of etiquette when men knew how to act and women react. Rules for the dating game have changed dramatically in the last few years and it certainly doesn't work as smoothly as is often portrayed in the movies.

To further complicate the process, the dating stage lasts longer in a person's life than ever before because people are marrying later. Then many people begin dating again following divorce or death of a spouse. Even though the game is played differently than a few years ago, the game is still being played and is here to stay. Let's look at the game, the players, new rules, and successful moves.

Pacing Relationships

Jennifer tearfully shared her story. "Bruce and I fell madly in love as soon as we met. For three months we spent every spare minute together. We were so in love it was difficult to keep our hands off each other because the physical attraction was so powerful. Then we began to argue a lot and get on each other's nerves. After discussing it, we concluded it was due to the sexual tension of our going so far but no farther. We thought the arguments would stop if we got married. For two months after we were married, everything was perfect. Then we began having more fights than ever and now we are miserable."

Married three months after they met, Jennifer and Bruce soon discovered that the initial rush of romantic feelings and sexual excitement doesn't continue forever. Four years and two children later, one disillusioned and angry couple separated.

Unfortunately Jennifer and Bruce are not unique. Many people marry before they have ridden out the wave of red-hot feelings and then they find themselves married to a totally unsuitable person. Society is quick to label this another marriage failure when in reality it is a dating failure. The tendency is to rush into marriage without first establishing a stable base for a relationship. There is no such thing as instant love. Strong lasting relationships must be paced over a long period of time where "getting to know you" is the major theme. This is why, for successful dating, I stress slowing down, taking your time, and looking carefully before you leap.

Stages in Dating Relationships

Outlined here are the seven stages in dating relationships. Note that each stage has a function and purpose in establishing a basis for the relationship. If any stage is rushed or skipped, there is a gap in the development of the relationship, and problems result.

Stage 1: Friendship

At the friendship stage, you get to know each other while participating in a nonromantic way in social, recreational, spiritual, and intellectual activities. Most of these are group, as opposed to couple, activities. The friendship stage is more casual and less emotional than the later dating stages, since no romantic or sexual overtones exist. *Dating* usually connotes romantic involvement. When a couple pairs off from the group, they are usually dating.

Friends often see each other at their worst—when upset about a traffic ticket, depressed over a job loss, covered with dirt and grime after cleaning out a garage. They get to know how each other responds to the ups and downs of life. There may be some flirting from time to time, a common occurrence in male-female relationships. But there is a fine line that friends choose not to cross.

Opposite-sex friends are comfortable doing what they would do with same-sex friends. Because it's not a dating relationship, friends don't feel the need to play games, and there are no sexual overtones. Friendships are infinitely less stressful than dating relationships. Often friends are more honest with each other than are lovers and it is possible for friends to become more emotionally intimate than lovers.

> *On the Trobriand Islands, if a woman wants to show a man that she is interested in him, she walks up to him and bites him.*
> *In Northern Syria, if a man wants to show a woman he is interested in her, he blows smoke in her face.*
>
> The Wrong Stuff

When Ann met Richard, marriage was hardly on her mind. After all, it was the first day of school for both of them and they were only six years old. All of their grade school and their high school years were spent at the same schools. They had the same teachers, studied many of the same subjects, played on the same volleyball team, and sang in the same church choir.

After a brief period of steady dating in the seventh grade, they broke up and drifted apart but never stopped being friends. This friendship continued into college where Richard began dating Ann again. He proposed to her a few months before graduation by hanging above the administration building a huge sign that read: "Ann, I love you. Will you marry me? Love, Richard." They were married following graduation.

Ann is happy to have a partner she has been friends with all her life and knows so well. A long list of places and events links their lives together in ways that other couples will never experience. Before they were ever married, each knew the security of a friendship where they could go with a problem and talk it out.

Not everyone can marry someone he has known from the first grade. But everyone can marry a friend. To do that we must slow down the process of relationship building and develop a strong friendship before romance is even considered.

Why go through all this friendship business? Why not convert every appealing candidate into romance as soon as possible? Most people don't have the talent or charisma for such conquests. And everyone benefits from moving into romance slowly. Love affairs that flare up instantly usually burn out just as fast. And it is much more likely in such relationships that you will be judged on superficial qualities like your appearance or body build rather than your character.

Strong dating relationships spring from strong friendships. The more you know about developing friendships the better you will be at the dating game.

Becoming friends before becoming romantically involved makes a lot of sense. If you fall in love too fast and it doesn't work out, you will rarely become friends again. If you take your time getting to know someone at the friendship level first and let love grow slowly and gradually, you are more likely to have a friend for life whether you marry this person or not.

Make no mistakes. It is harder to remain friends than lovers. The easy thing to do when you find someone you are attracted to, is to shift into high gear, give it all you've got, and gun it. It is infinitely more difficult to take your foot off the gas pedal and move slowly when there are no curves, detours, or road blocks in sight. But choosing the fast, easy route will rarely build a relationship that lasts because when conflicts arise the tendency is to choose the easy way—walking out.

Stage 2: Casual Dating

Two friends now move away from the group to engage in couple activities. They have learned through their friendship that they share many interests and that they enjoy being together. The pleasure of friendship is simply extended into couple activities.

Bert has several women friends he enjoys dating. One of them makes a great skiing partner, and another is a scuba diver. He chooses to be with another woman when he needs a listener. And he often takes another friend to social gatherings because of her life-of-the-party personality.

Sue prefers this kind of dating also. She and a coworker share a passion for classical music and they attend concerts together. She and another male friend enjoy mountain biking dates.

Neither Sue nor Bert is interested in a long-term romantic commitment at the present. Each is comfortable with more casual relationships that fill the need for companionship without heavy emotional responsibility. Both are up front with those they date about other dating partners.

At this stage two people date for the pleasure of sharing an enjoyable activity with a member of the opposite sex. Both are free to date others. The degree of emotional commitment between them is low or even nonexistent. They do not consider themselves to be in love. Pleasant times are shared along with a friendship that *may* hold promise for the future.

Should they continue to enjoy each other's company the relationship will likely begin to include hand holding and other romantic gestures.

I recommend that a couple remain at the friendship and casual dating stages for six to twelve months, getting acquainted with each other's likes and dislikes and learning about backgrounds, habits, and behaviors. If what they learn at this unhurried pace checks out with what they're looking for, they can slowly move into the next stage. It is possible to remain friends for months and even years without becoming romantically involved.

Stage 3: Special Dating

Special dating is an in-between stage that means there is a growing emotional attachment between the two but they have not yet reached the commitment required in a steady relationship. They are spending more time together but are not yet dating steadily.

Stage 4: Steady Dating

In steady dating there is an understanding or agreement between two people that they will not date others and they see each other more often than in casual dating. For the first time, words like _commitment_ and _exclusive_ come into play.

Adult singles usually attach more significance to steady dating than do teenagers. And they should. Steady dating for the mature couple is associated with interest in sharing a future together. It provides an opportunity to look each other over carefully with no commitment to marriage yet. This is an important stage during which a relationship can be thoroughly tested because of the amount of time the couple is spending together. It shows if the two people involved are able to remain committed to one relationship. This is important to know before marriage is considered. At this stage a couple thinks they are in love but still may not be certain.

In steady dating two people develop confidence and competence in interacting with a person of the opposite sex over an extended period of time. They also get to know themselves better, as well as how they are perceived by the opposite sex.

Many personality traits can be observed during this stage. Is he a good listener or conversationalist? Does he have a good sense of humor? What about manners, thoughtfulness, ability to concentrate? It's during this stage that one can observe character traits such as dependability, spirituality, and maturity. There will be opportunities to discuss values and goals for the future. Communication skills can and should be carefully evaluated. Does he hear what I am saying or does he only listen? Is he able to hear the feelings behind my words? Does he pout or use the silent treatment? Can hurt feelings be addressed openly or are they stuffed and avoided? How is anger handled and conflicts solved? Can differences of opinion be negotiated to satisfactory conclusions? Is one always winning and the other losing? Is there a "we" or a "me" feeling when we are together?

When steady dating is used to its full potential, it provides a serious trial period during which a couple can make intelligent decisions regarding their compatibility. It can form a natural bridge to the stages of pre-engagement and formal engagement.

Stage 5: Pre-Engagement

Pre-engagement is the period between steady dating and formal engagement when a couple begins discussing the possibility of marriage. At this stage the couple talks about a permanent relationship—"someday." Someday when I get that promotion or when we can afford it or when circumstances that prevent it now allow it. All talk and plans are tentative. Their understanding is private and personal rather than final or binding. The talk, however, generally sounds something like this: "Someday, when we are married we'll . . . Someday when we have kids . . . Someday after we save enough money . . . Someday we'll have a house like . . ."

During this stage a couple can take an in-depth look at whether their lifestyles and personalities are compatible enough for marriage. The couple is more sure than they were at the steady dating stage that they are made for each other and that they have found genuine love, but nothing is binding at this point.

The couple test and retest their values, goals, and future plans. Much of what used to be discussed only during the formal engagement period is opened here for scrutiny. This approach should make the engagement more meaningful as well as reduce the number of broken engagements. It also can take the pressure off couples who are dating steadily but are not ready to announce their intentions to marry.

It is during this stage, before a couple formally announces their engagement, that I recommend relationship counseling by a pastor or counselor. This is when a couple can take a serious look at their compatibility and their ability to communicate. A couple's ability to communicate is the single most important contributor to a stable and satisfying marriage. The most important goal of any stage 5 couple is to improve communication skills.

> *During World War II, Reverend Canon Bill Cook and his fiancée, Helen, exchanged six thousand love letters over the span of four and one-half years.*
> The 1989 Guinness Book of World Records

This is the last period—before a formal commitment has been announced—to bail out of a relationship without making it really uncomfortable for everyone involved.

Stage 6: Formal Engagement

The formal engagement follows the "someday" talk of stage 5. It brings a deep sense of commitment and belonging that doesn't come with going steady or pre-engagement.

There are several things that separate the formal engagement from the pre-engagement stage. A formal engagement announcement serves as public notice to friends and family that a couple intend to marry. It provides an opportunity for others to adjust to the fact that a new family unit will soon form and a new member will join the extended family. The public announcement tends to strengthen the commitment. The more people who know about the engagement, the more likely the couple is to follow through and marry. Thus a secret engagement is really no engagement at all.

Traditionally the prospective groom presents a gift to the prospective bride to solemnize the engagement. This gift is a symbol of their commitment to each other. The gift may be dishes, an heirloom, a piece of furniture, a watch, but usually it's an engagement ring. This gift of love further strengthens the couple's commitment.

The third thing that makes an engagement formal is that the wedding date is set and wedding plans begin. Becoming engaged can be so satisfying and thrilling in itself that many couples do not pay enough attention to what it really stands for in relationship to their future, but engagement is not an end in itself. It's a commitment to marry. Therefore, plans for a wedding need to proceed. An engagement with no wedding date in sight destroys the value of engagement.

The engagement stage should not be long because an engaged couple's desire for intimacy will increase. Expressions of affection will become more intense because they are in a transition period from courtship to marriage. Because of this urgency to fulfill the natural desire for unrestricted intimacy, I recommend short engagements of six to nine months. Church weddings usually require at least six months of planning.

If a couple have spent two years getting to know each other before the engagement, the short engagement period will be sufficient. This period is another opportunity to discuss the future and lay plans for the first year of marriage. Many things may have been discussed previously, but now the couple will talk more intimately and specifically. This is the last opportunity to check out the future partner before being locked in for life. The couple have already done some investigating or they would not have reached the engagement stage, but now they check and recheck their evaluations. This is the time to bring out any unresolved differences or reveal any hidden secrets.

Remember that engagement is not a sealed contract that forever links a couple's destiny. It is possible that as a couple get to know each other better during engagement, they will decide not to marry. This is hardly an unheard of phenomenon. As many as 40 to 50 percent of all engagements are broken. As difficult as a broken engagement is, it is better than a broken marriage.

The most important task to be accomplished during engagement is not the planning of a wedding, but having premarital counseling with a qualified pastor or professional counselor. The previously married usually attempt to bypass this step. One pastor suggested to a couple who were planning marriage that they come in for premarital counseling. "We don't need that," the man responded. "We've both been married before."

All the more reason for a checkup before marriage—to settle any unresolved issues from the past that might haunt the future. Every couple should have a minimum of six counseling sessions before marriage.

Stage 7: Marriage

The seventh and final stage is marriage. This may surprise you. Many people don't think of the dating relationship continuing into marriage, but the friendship and love established during dating is the basis for a strong relationship in marriage. Marriage is final and binding. It is different than the previous six stages in that legal procedures and courts are necessary to dissolve the relationship through divorce. It is similar in that it should be a continuation of the roman-

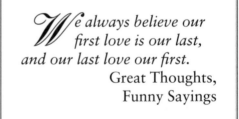

We always believe our first love is our last, and our last love our first.
Great Thoughts,
Funny Sayings

tic phase of the courtship process characterized by affection, attention, respect, courtesy, and fun together.

Notice the six distinct and different stages prior to marriage. Unfortunately couples often go through these stages out of sequence. They jump to steady dating or pre-engagement and ignore the need for friendship first. So eager are they to find love, they skip the preliminaries and jump into romance. Frequently I ask married couples if they consider themselves to be best friends. Such an idea sounds bizarre to many because they never thought about whether they liked each other. They just fell in love. But liking each other and being friends go a long way in contributing to happiness in marriage. All the romantic stuff does not necessarily produce lasting love if an enduring friendship has not first been established.

The Two-Year Rule

I have found that adult singles, especially the previously married, tend to act in haste and marry too quickly. I recommend that every couple date for two years prior to engagement. One whole year should be spent at stages 1, 2, and 3, slowly and carefully nurturing a friendship first. During the second year the "masks" begin to slip and character and personality flaws emerge that had been successfully hidden until then.

Many people can successfully mask negative tendencies for a year. Only rarely can such game playing go beyond that, however. Therefore, when a couple rushes into marriage too quickly, they have not allowed sufficient time for the masks to slip. They are marrying a virtual stranger, someone who will likely turn out to be stranger than they ever wanted to know. Rapid acceleration of relationships is so exciting that romantic feelings stay alive when they should begin fading. As the euphoria intensifies, the thrill of being a twosome and doing enjoyable things together blinds the couple to reality. The question is not, Does my loved one have faults? But rather, Can I live comfortably with the faults I now see? Marrying in haste, without taking sufficient time to check a person out, is jumping into a relationship based on assumptions. Assumptions make appalling marriage partners.

I have taught hundreds of courtship and marriage seminars, read hundreds of books on the family, written twenty books myself, and counseled hundreds of couples whose marriages were in serious trouble. I know a major contributing factor to the unhappiness of most couples was skipping steps and rushing too fast into marriage.

Researchers at Kansas State University have proved my point valid. In their survey of middle-aged wives "a strong correlation was found between length of time spent dating their current spouses and current marital satisfaction." The researchers noted that "couples who had dated for more than two years scored consistently high on marital satisfaction, while couples who had dated for shorter periods scored in a wide range from very high to very low."[1] The likelihood of experiencing a high level of marital satisfaction is greatly enhanced by dating two years or longer.

Nothing gets my attention faster than hearing a couple talk about marriage who have not completed the two-year dating time frame. They are about to pledge "till death do us part" and have seriously underestimated the need for a strong relationship and positive communication to weather future financial crises, bouts of sickness, and misunderstandings.

Bill and Nina met at a singles meeting at their church. Afterward they went out for something to eat. "We talked for hours," Nina says. "I'd never met anyone that I could share with quite so fast. That first night I knew him better than all the other guys I've dated put together. I told him things about myself I'd never shared with anyone. We dated every night for a week and then Bill proposed. I'd never met anyone like him before. I knew it was right and accepted."

Bill also remembers that first week. "Nina was the most intelligent and beautiful girl I'd met in years. I could hardly take my eyes off her. I wanted to touch her and hold her. She had real sex appeal, let me tell you! We saw each other every day. I was hooked. I never loved anyone the way I loved her. When she said she loved me too, I knew this was it! We had to get married."

And Bill and Nina got married—one month after they met. Four months later they separated and filed for divorce. What happened? This couple made the mistake of moving from stage 1 to stage 7 of the dating game in four weeks! It can't be done without serious consequences.

The two-year rule is applicable to the previously married also. I have seen some happily married couples in second marriages. But those who are happy the second time around are most often those who didn't rush to develop the relationship.

Some of the biggest fiascoes I've witnessed involved previously married individuals who thought because they were "experienced," they could skip all the "kid stuff." "After all," they declare, "we're not teenagers."

Not only do divorced people attempt to short-circuit the getting-to-know-you process, but so do those who have lost a spouse to death. Men, especially, are less likely to understand and deal properly with their emotions after the death of a spouse and they hurry into new marriages to shortcut the grief process.

I am convinced that every couple regardless of their ages, circumstances, or experience need to take two full years to evaluate their readiness for marriage. When they do, they will have a significantly higher likelihood of making a good choice. The most important advice I give in this book can be summed up in three words: TAKE YOUR TIME.

The Difficulty of Pacing Relationships

Progressing too rapidly in a relationship causes two problems for a couple. First, there is a strong possibility that the couple will not slow the pace sufficiently to develop the skills necessary to maintain a long-term relationship. Relational skills such as communication, settling conflicts, or dealing with power struggles will likely be untested. Immature couples tend to resolve their conflicts in bed, especially if this pattern was learned in the past. Their relationship lacks depth and the first hint of difficulty signals a serious threat.

The second problem in rushing the stages is that there is insufficient time for infatuation, romantic glow, or existing "masks" to slip and reality to set in.

Developing a relationship with someone of the opposite sex is so electrifying it becomes difficult to spread intimacy-building over a time period sufficient for real depth to develop. A compelling desire to spend as much time together as possible immediately propels the couple toward physical intimacy and commitment.

Because of the intense attraction between the sexes, it seems more exciting to be "in love" and all that goes with it than to exercise self-discipline, slow things down, think things through, and pace the relationship properly. It is more stimulating to belong to someone, be in love, or be engaged than it is to be "only friends." There is a sense of security in "belonging" to someone.

Sometimes women make more of a relationship than really exists due to a deep inner longing to be special to someone, to be loved, and to establish a home. A man sometimes pushes the relationship to obtain sexual privileges. "After all," he urges, "we love each other and we plan to marry."

Each with a hidden agenda attempts, in a backwards way, to know the other. They become sexually involved and later attempt to build a friendship. Be smarter than such people. Go forward through a relationship, not backward.

4

Great Dates

Where to Go and What to Do

Developing physical intimacy is infinitely more exciting and less work than developing intimacy at the emotional, spiritual, and friendship levels. This makes physical intimacy more difficult to control. But it can be controlled if you choose your dating activities carefully. Some activities build relationships slowly but surely at the friendship level; others rapidly hurl couples toward physical intimacy. An afternoon spent exploring a historic town is more constructive than a day spent cuddling on a blanket at the beach.

"It's not asking a girl out that bothers me," a tanned, athletic male confided to a friend. "It's where to take her. I always fall back on the same thing—a movie and something to eat. I find such dates boring and I'm afraid the women do too!"

There are two kinds of dates: the spectator date, during which you watch and/or listen to entertainment; and the participation date, during which you are actively involved in recreation.

Spectator Dates

Spectator dates include going to movies, plays, concerts, and sports events, watching TV or videos, and listening to music. Spectator dates are popular because most people enjoy spectator entertainment and on first dates there is less stress involved in trying to keep the conversation going. Furthermore, literally everyone already knows how to be a spectator—sit and watch. That's another plus.

On the down side, spectator dates can be expensive. And the main purpose of dating—getting to know one another—is defeated since watching someone else perform allows for little interaction between the two people on the date.

Watching TV or videos or listening to music are particularly dangerous because they involve being alone, usually with the lights low. Many consecutive hours spent alone in spectator dates weakens resistance to sexual temptation and rapidly hurls a couple toward premature expressions of sexual intimacy. Several short spectator dates are safer than a long or all-day date.

Participation Dates

The second type, the participation date, includes such activities as playing miniature golf or tennis, canoeing, sailing, hiking, visiting a museum or a zoo, and doing crafts such as woodworking. Such dates are seldom boring. Instead, participating together in an activity encourages the expression of creative abilities, reaffirms feelings of worth, usually costs less, and allows the couple to explore likes and dislikes. Each can develop new skills and abilities as well as gain insights into the other. Participation dates also provide fewer opportunities for sexual temptation.

Participation dates require creativity and initiative. For many people, planning an activity may require more effort than they're willing to give. Some people are too self-conscious for many participation dates. They don't think their skills are good enough. With a little ingenuity, however, everyone can come up with activities they can enjoy.

Here are some ideas. Some require athletic ability but many don't. Sports such as cross-country skiing, tennis, golf, swimming, Ping-Pong, croquet, horseshoes, roller blading, jogging, and hiking. Do-at-home activities such as craft projects; making ice cream, bread, or a gourmet dinner; board games; and reading together. Or explore a new town, go picture taking, ride bikes, throw a Frisbee, collect shells from the beach, pass out Christian literature, and visit a nursing home.

You can spend money to make a date unforgettable but it isn't necessary. Designing a creative date with a personal touch is the secret. Here are some blockbuster ideas for the more adventuresome:

- Purchase outlandish outfits at a thrift store and take a stroll through the park stopping to eat a picnic lunch.
- Rent a bicycle built for two, decorate it, and ride it through a local park or scenic area. Invent some games to play while riding.
- Refinish a piece of furniture.
- Plan, purchase, then cook and serve a meal for family or friends.
- Make your own kites and fly them.
- Plan a tour of an airplane factory, alligator farm, or television station.
- Produce your own video. Invite friends over for a premiere showing. Serve popcorn.

Since participation dates offer more advantages than do spectator dates, they should make up a larger portion of your dating life. You may not always be able to handle one for a first date, but if you can—go for it!

A couple can control the progression of their relationship when they choose their dating activities wisely by often including participation dates and by limiting their time alone together.

How and Where to Find a Date

The secret to finding a dating partner and eventually getting married is meeting a large number of prospects. The larger the number of prospects the greater the likelihood of meeting someone compatible. A prospect is anyone of the opposite sex who is single, available for a relationship, living reasonably close by, and committed to similar values.

Unfortunately most people meet only a small number of prospects and wonder why they never find the right person. These people end up alone, dateless, and often depressed.

Three Rules for Meeting Prospects

Most singles could double or triple the number of prospects they meet each year by following three simple rules:

1. _Get out of the house._ It will do little good to stay home day and night hoping and praying you'll meet someone special. The love of your life rarely knocks on the front door searching for you—unless you expect to fall in love with the mailperson or the UPS driver.

> _In the late 1700s, humans were not the only ones to dress modestly. Pianos did too. Certain American ladies decided it wasn't right for a piano to display its exposed legs. So they made specially designed pants to cover the legs of their pianos._
>
> The Natural History of Love

2. *Go where the fish are.* If you were a fisherman, you wouldn't go to a neighbor's pool to reel in a big one. You'd go to a lake or river where fish are plentiful. The same holds true in the dating game. You must use the right lure (we'll talk about this later in the chapter but self-esteem is the most important) and go where the prospects are. The biggest "sin" of the dateless is to wait for the phone to ring while complaining she never meets anyone interesting! You must get out and involved. Make a list of activities you enjoy. Then get involved in one or more of them where you are likely to meet members of the opposite sex. Guys should go where there are women—jazzercise, aerobics, swimming classes, or church. A woman looking for prospects can forget aerobics and head for the fitness club. Plenty of men are on racquetball courts and softball teams. They may be at high school football fields where fathers hang out to see their sons play. They're checking the ticker tape at brokerage firms or along jogging paths. Your chances increase as you select the right arenas.

3. *Initiate contact.* If you sit around waiting for others to initiate contact with you, you'll have few dates. But if you risk falling on your face, you just may find the love of your life. When you initiate contact, you're in a better position because you have some control of the situation. It may be difficult but it's the only way to develop relationships with those people you've found appealing.

Five Ways to Meet Someone Special

Here are the five best ways to meet someone. Remember, when you get out of the house and go to the right places, the next step is to initiate contact.

1. *Through friends.* From one survey of three thousand singles it was found that one-third meet their dating partners through their friends.[1] It may well pay off to cultivate a wide circle of friends and nurture those friendships. Each of your friends has friends. Sooner or later these friends will have social gatherings—where you will probably meet new

people. You can't depend on friends to find you dates, but having a wide circle of friends in various places increases your odds of meeting someone special.

Throw a party for your friends and ask them to bring along new friends. Invite new acquaintances you'd like to get to know better. Make it potluck if you can't afford more. Also, you should take a fresh look at your neighbors. A great possibility may live in the apartment upstairs! This is called networking. Networking is nothing more than utilizing every opportunity to meet someone new through the people you know. Networking goes beyond calling a friend and saying, "I'm really lonely. Do you know anyone who is looking for a date?" It means being friendly, staying in touch with friends, and letting them know you are looking for introductions. Married friends are often especially happy to recommend someone they know. Generally speaking they recognize whether a person is marriage material or not.

2. _At the office._ One-tenth of the singles in this survey met their partners at work. This has an advantage because you already know them. You see them daily, which gives you time to observe their work habits and their talents and abilities as well as how they interact with others. You already have things in common to discuss. But there's a downside. When a breakup occurs you still have to face each other daily. And no matter how discreet you are, people do gossip.

3. _In church, clubs, or classes._ These can provide excellent opportunities to meet someone who shares an interest that means a lot to you. Join as many groups as you can. Groups might include a hiking club, the PTA, a choir, language classes, a fitness group, night school, or a book club. Be adventuresome and join something new.

Kate was no raving beauty or brilliant conversationalist but she wanted to break out of her cocoon and make friends. She signed up for an evening Chinese cooking class. There she met some new people—both men and women. After the class was over the group decided to meet once a week for an ethnic feast. There often was a lot of interaction while planning the menu before each meal as well as during the meal itself. Kate wasn't sure she wanted to become romantically involved with any of the men in the group, but even if that never happened, she had developed some valuable new friendships. And she was increasing her odds of meeting someone special, since each of these people had friends.

4. *At parties or social occasions.* These can be especially beneficial when both individuals know the host. Accept as many invitations as possible and enjoy yourself!

5. *Through the course of everyday life.* Be on the alert! That someone special could be at the bus stop, in line at the supermarket, in the waiting room at the auto repair shop—the possibilities are limitless.

Checking Out the Personals

It's not so much where you find someone as what you make of the opportunity when it arises that makes the difference. Those who are enthusiastic about life and have many interests are those who will be appealing to the opposite sex. Every time you embark on a new enterprise, you multiply your opportunities. Staying home and watching TV leads to isolation and loneliness.

You may want to try a different approach. From coast to coast respectable Christian publications are accepting personal ads. You advertise, then pick and choose the responses you will answer. When writing your ad you'll need to make a list of your assets (physical, financial, and

Some people went to extremes to keep males and females separate in England during the late 1800s. For example, Lady Gough's Book of Etiquette *even suggested that books by male authors should be kept apart from books by female authors.*

Sacrifice

social). You'll also want to list qualities that are the most important to you in a date. Advertise in a publication that can bring the greatest number of responses from near where you live. It can take several months for a response. In the meantime, get a good photo of yourself ready to mail out and write some snappy replies.

Video dating services have opened up a world of eligible men and women interested in dating. Look for ads in respectable Christian publications. This can be an expensive option but may be worth it. You will first need to fill out a personality profile. Then a taping session is scheduled. That's the hard part. After that it gets to be fun. From your personality profile, potential dating partners are matched with you. You view their videos and select several people you might like to meet. These people come into the video dating service and read your personality profile, see your picture, and view your video. If the person wishes to meet you, she is given your last name and phone number. When that person calls, you take it from there. Video dating services offer several advantages in that you can see a person's video and make judgments regarding appearance, nonverbal behaviors, and tone of voice before actually meeting her. The person's responses to questions can reveal a lot about personality and values.

One woman said in the first year of her membership in a video dating service, she selected more than thirty men and was selected by almost as many. She said no to many as soon as she saw their tapes and evaluated their appearance and what they were saying. She said yes to a few she initially liked and later ruled out as prospects. Then one day, on the thirty-seventh try, she had a date with a man who eventually became her husband.

Being Selective

It is only natural to desire attractive and popular people to date. But many men or women make great dates even though they wear glasses, are short, overweight, quiet, or are not beauty contest material. Sometimes the best "finds" haven't blossomed yet. Avoid being shallow and looking only for physical beauty. Some interesting people come in plain packaging. Try one!

And remember, the main purpose of dating is to establish friendship—not marriage!

Strategies for Successful Dating

First dates can be quite traumatic. You may be frantic over what to wear and how to be appealing. You may worry that the evening could be a total disaster. But in the back of your mind, you wonder if this date could lead to marriage. With all this going on no wonder you're nervous! On the date you'll likely be anxious, tongue-tied, and possibly even clumsy. To ease first-date jitters, here are some success secrets.

Daytime is better for first dates than evenings. A first date should be informal and nonthreatening. A picnic in the park with a Frisbee or lunch at an outdoor café would be perfect. This kind of date offers more opportunity to chat and get to know each other than does watching a movie in a dark theater. This is how you can find out if you have anything in common. So get outdoors into a daylight activity. Go for a walk or a swim, ride bikes, or play tennis.

Set a time limit on your date. People tend to overestimate how long a first date should be. They think that spending many hours together will make the relationship more special faster. But dates, especially early in the relationship, should have a beginning and ending time set in advance. Then if it isn't working you can more easily change your plans.

Meet in a public place, unless you have already developed a friendship with this person. A restaurant or coffee shop is a good place to meet for a first date. And each person should drive his or her own car. That way you are free to leave when you wish. If the date doesn't go well, be prepared for a fast getaway with a polite but well-rehearsed speech like: "This doesn't look like it's going anywhere. Let's not waste each other's time. Thanks for meeting me. I've got to go now." And leave. You owe this person nothing more than this.

Be on time. If you say you'll be at a place or ready at a certain time and you aren't, you are being rude. It is no longer considered "cute" to keep a man waiting. It is just as improper for a man to be late. If you are going to be late, call your date and inform her. Being late for a date conveys a message: This event is not important enough for me to arrange my time accordingly. A recent survey of one thousand Americans revealed that on a first date, the best impression comes from the date being on time (52 percent). Fifty-two percent also made an impression by complimenting their date's appearance or personality.

Be mature. Whether you are thirty-three, forty-three, or fifty-three, be mature. Have respect for the other person and yourself. One thing that this means is no sex. There is no place for sexual intimacy before you and your date have achieved emotional intimacy. This is backwards.

Relax. Concentrate on trying to put your date at ease. Think of her as a friend rather than a romantic partner. Then you'll be able to relax.

Dee was terribly nervous over her first date with Dan. She did not need to worry. He was an excellent conversationalist and encouraged her to talk. This first date was followed by many more. Much later Dan told Dee he was a nervous wreck on their first date, yet Dee knew nothing about it, because Dan had helped her feel at ease.

Be fun to be with. Contribute to the date by being fun. Don't expect to sit back and be entertained without contributing something to the evening to make it memorable. Allow yourself to act a little crazy as long as it is in good taste. Join in with what your date has planned even if you feel a little self-conscious. Participate in the activities as long as they don't conflict with your principles. If they do, bow out gracefully, offering an acceptable alternative. And don't complain when something doesn't go as planned.

If you did your best and things didn't go well, it doesn't mean that you have to scrap the friendship. First dates can be tense. If you think there's a chance that the relationship might work, call and say something like this, "Things didn't go as well yesterday as I hoped they might. I was really nervous. But I enjoyed your company and would like to see you again."

Great Date Traits

One study revealed that 90 percent of the singles polled felt they were "good" dates. However, when the same males and females rated each other, they were quite critical of the other's dating abilities! Another informal survey of likes and dislikes among single adults found the most common turnoffs for both men and women were bragging, gloominess, insincerity, and "lines." Both sexes also agreed they were most attracted by someone who was smiling and self-confident and showed interest in getting to know them.

According to nationwide research, the qualities that single adults consider "very important" in a date are listed in the following table.

Qualities	Percentage of men who value this quality	Percentage of women who value this quality
Integrity, sensitivity, kindness, understanding	65%	81%
Sense of humor	60	52
Intelligence, perceptivity	39	52

Qualities	Percentage of men who value this quality	Percentage of women who value this quality
Common interests, talents, backgrounds	26	32
Skill as a lover	28	17
Physical attractiveness	29	17
Money, status, and position	10	15

The authors state: "On the list of most important attractions—above physical appearance, above intelligence, above money or expertise in the bedroom, above all priorities but one—comes a sense of humor. Among singles of all ages there is little variation of opinion on this issue. . . . [They] claim sense of humor to be a very important or at least a somewhat important attraction."[2]

For those who are interested in being terrific dates rather than only dating terrific persons, the following are some surefire strategies.

Show interest in your date. Attempt to learn beforehand one interesting thing about your date, such as a hobby or talent. This will give you a better basis for communicating. When you encourage your date to talk about her interests, you can gain a tremendous amount of information that will help you evaluate the future of the relationship.

Be enthusiastic. Without being pushy, obnoxious, or forward, let your date know you are looking forward to the occasion.

Adopt a positive mind-set. Think about having an enjoyable time. If you think you are going to have fun, you are more likely to enjoy the occasion.

Wear an outfit that makes you look and feel terrific. This gives your self-worth a boost. You can forget your self-consciousness and concentrate on making your date feel comfortable.

Learn techniques for being a good conversationalist. Beginning a conversation is the most difficult part, but it can be handled by asking open-ended questions that are nonthreatening and not too personal. Try something like this: "So you grew up in Wisconsin. Tell me about your favorite part of Wisconsin"; or, "What's your favorite way to spend your free time?" Talking about what the other enjoys catapults you into the center of her world and puts your date at ease. Lori tried this with Stan and genuinely enjoyed listening to him tell about his skiing adventures. She had a few of her own to add and they laughed till they cried. After establishing a common bond around skiing, it seemed they could talk about anything. A good conversationalist can almost talk her way right into the heart of another person.

Be a good listener. Show interest in the topics your date brings up. Raise your eyebrows, nod your head in agreement, smile a lot. As your partner talks, you can relax. You don't have to do all the talking and will be considered a better date if you don't. Learning to listen is an art.

Be prepared to talk about something interesting for ten minutes. Memorize a funny story or anecdote for use when you need it. You shouldn't dominate the conversation but you do need to be able to keep it moving when necessary. Your date shouldn't have to do all the talking.

Talk very little about yourself. Tell only the things you're comfortable telling. Don't talk about your ex. Be prepared to respond to direct questions about a previous marriage by saying, "When I know you a little better, I'll tell you . . ."

Be yourself. If your date asks if you prefer Mexican or Chinese food, state your preference. You'll speed up the getting-to-know-you phase and your relationship will be more honest if you make your preferences and interests known. With practice you'll be able to say graciously what you prefer.

Let your date know if you are having a good time. If you aren't, at least be polite!

Let your self-assurance show. Feeling good about yourself makes it easier to attract others. From time to time we all project negative feelings. That's normal. But if you habitually feel bad about yourself, others will be able to tell by the expression on your face, the way you carry yourself, and the way you talk. Then the message you project is "stay away." Don't grumble and complain. Don't run yourself or others down, which shows low self-esteem. If your image invites others to get to know you, you're more likely to have dating partners who will ask you out again.

Don't let bad habits creep into your dating behavior. Just as you can develop bad habits while typing or exercising, you can allow bad habits to develop in your dating life and ruin things. Talking too much; being loud; acting possessive, jealous, or anxious; and not maintaining eye contact are some habits that can sabotage your dating relationship.

Successful dating depends largely on personality, behavior, and appearance. To be a really terrific date you need to ask yourself some questions: When with friends how do I act? How do I sound? How do I treat my friends? Would I like to date me? Your response to these questions to a large extent determines your dating future. Practice behaviors that enhance a relationship, so that they will come naturally.

As attractive, sensitive, and pleasant as you may be, keep in mind you'll not hit it off with everyone. Little good will come from whipping yourself for every rejection or for every date that doesn't go anywhere. Do see if there is anything you can learn from each encounter.

If you are having trouble getting a second date or maintaining a relationship over time, you need date coaching. There may be a course in personality development at your local community college that would be helpful. You may want to counsel with a professional counselor. This could include testing to obtain a personality profile. Then you know the specific personality traits that need work. Many people find a support group helpful. Through a group experience, you are able to see yourself as you really are.

A Word to Lonely Hearts

You are reasonably good looking; you have a good job, a wide circle of friends; and you are active at church. In other words, you have your life in order. Except for one thing—no dates and there haven't been any for some time. That was okay for a while. You were finishing your education and building your career. There was little time for romance. But now that you are ready for romance, it eludes you and you wonder what you are doing wrong. You aren't interested in the people who pursue you and when you find someone you're interested in, the feelings aren't mutual. Sometimes you wonder if you are too picky. It seems that prospects are either too old or too young. Some seem too nice and others act like jerks. Some want to tell you how to run your life. And others don't want a commitment.

> *In 1837, an Englishman sued a girl because she bit him in the nose when he kissed her against her will. As it turned out, though, she won the case. According to the judge, "When a man kisses a woman against her will, she is fully entitled to bite his nose, if she so pleases."*
>
> Robert Ebisch

You've made a real effort to stay in circulation. You signed up for a class at the university and took up a hobby. You go to lots of parties and are involved in your church's singles activities. Still you often spend your evenings alone.

If this sounds familiar, you are in the same boat as thousands of other intelligent, successful adults who just can't seem to find the right partner. Many singles think that being alone is worse than a prison sentence and that companionship is necessary to satisfy basic human needs. They think that being alone makes them abnormal and they feel desperate to find a life's partner.

You may be feeling desperate. You may feel like David did when he wrote these verses:

> I am bowed down and brought very low;
>   all day long I go about mourning. . . .
>   there is no health in my body.
> I am feeble and utterly crushed;
>   I groan in anguish of heart.
> All my longings lie open before you, O Lord;
>   my sighing is not hidden from you.
> My heart pounds, my strength fails me;
>   even the light has gone from my eyes.
> My friends and companions avoid me
>   because of my wounds;
>   my neighbors stay far away.
>
> Psalm 38:6–11

Does that sound like where you have been? Or currently are? Then give it to Jesus, Great Healer of all wounds. Let Him take it from you. He can take your painful loneliness and turn it into enjoyable, fruitful, and productive experience if you will allow Him.

David did. In the previous verses he said he would wait for the Lord's answer. Confessing his iniquity, he pled with the Lord to be near and help him.

Being single does not brand or label you. A social misfit you are not. However, if you continue to give in to feelings of desperation, you will make irrational decisions and bad choices. Satan, who as your enemy rejoices in your panic and desperation, wants those feelings to persist. He'll use your panic to lead you into destructive patterns of behavior.

It's important to come to terms with being single. It's a lifestyle that's okay. Then you must deal with your loneliness. Loneliness is a feeling. Both marrieds and singles can experience it. It's a part of life. But to desperately chase after anything or anyone to avoid loneliness is a drastic mistake. There are things worse than loneliness.

Recognize your need for friends and regular social interaction and plan an interesting round of activities with both single and married friends. Guard against going to the opposite extreme so that you are alone too much and become introverted.

Reach out to others rather than expecting them to reach out to you. You might prefer to spend Saturday night with a significant other. But since most singles meet their dating partners through friends, you can enjoy your friends and increase your odds of meeting someone at the same time. Now you'll find that your lonely times are bearable and aloneness isn't so bad after all!

Part 3

Breaking Up
without Breaking Down

5

Facing Reality

Relationships That Can't Endure

Sometimes it is healthier to break off a relationship than to keep it going. Many times singles become involved in relationships that signal "danger ahead!" but somehow, when emotionally involved, they fail to see the danger or they close their eyes to it.

When we become emotionally involved in a situation, we frequently lose perspective. When the love juices start flowing, romantic notions start wheeling through the head and temporary insanity takes over! Do yourself a favor. Squarely face and carefully evaluate all danger signals in your relationship. If the obstacles are too big and if there is potential disaster, end the relationship now. If you are too emotionally dependent to evaluate it truthfully or end it alone, enlist the help of a counselor. But get out and the sooner the better.

> *Most girls find that the one quality they admire most in a man is availability.*
>
> Great Thoughts,
> Funny Sayings

When a relationship is destructive or leading to a dead end, you must end it. Let's focus on some circumstances that indicate these kinds of relationships. This list will act as a starter for sluggish hearts who may hate to face reality.

Danger Signal 1: Ineffectively Dealing with Conflict

A real test for any potential love match is how conflict is handled. Any couple who wants a harmonious relationship and a lasting marriage is going to have to learn how to manage conflict constructively. If they do not, their relationship will become a garbage dump of unresolved disagreements. The litter will keep their relationship from moving ahead. The ability of a couple to manage conflict is more important than how much in love they are, how compatible they are, or any other factor. People divorce due more to their inability to resolve conflict than to any other reason. It is vital to carefully evaluate your ability as a couple to manage conflict.

Showing Respect

An important factor in conflict resolution is respect. Do the two people show respect for each other as well as for themselves when speaking? If each respects the other, they will listen even if they do not like or approve of what the other is saying. Gestures, touching, facial expressions, and the amount of eye contact maintained are all indications of how much respect the two people have for each other. If there is the foundation of respect, the skills required for learning conflict resolution can be easily mastered. If respect is not present, skills are useless.

82

Arguing and Fighting

Couples who cannot deal effectively with their differences without arguments and fights should not consider marriage. Some arguing and fighting during an ongoing relationship is normal. If a couple never disagrees or argues, they are not really being themselves and have probably not learned to interact honestly with each other. But there is certainly such a thing as too many disagreements, especially if they are loud, long, or continuous. Even well-matched couples may have a series of misunderstandings, but, overall, if the fights outnumber the periods of peace, there is something to worry about.

Suppressing Feelings

Some people deal with conflict by ignoring it. They refuse to discuss a problem or may even deny that a problem exists. These people will show their displeasure in other ways, however, through the silent treatment, pouting, emotionally shutting out the partner, or punishing him in other ways. Such tactics are terribly destructive and make it next to impossible to resolve the conflict.

Jim grew up in a home where anger was suppressed. His family and his church rigidly taught that anger was a sin. This rule was enforced in spoken and unspoken ways. If Jim dared to express anger, he was severely punished. One day he threw his books on the floor after an exasperating day at school. This cost him a stern lecture on self-control and an evening in his room without supper. Other displays of temper got him a beating with a belt. Jim learned to suppress his anger and ignore conflict. Jim is married now, and friends would rate his marriage as happy because of the outward appearance of harmony and the lack of obvious friction. But Jim and his wife are painfully aware of emotional distance between them. Jim refuses to deal with any conflict they have. As a result he suffers from high blood pressure and is impotent.

Anger

Denise was raised by parents who could be manipulated. She could always get her way by throwing a fit of temper. She has always used displays of temper to try to control all her relationships. And when she's angry, she'll say anything, no matter how much it may hurt the other person. With her husband her words are often hostile, bitter, and nasty. Sometimes she goes beyond sharp words to violent shouting and threats.

People who use anger in this manner feel a sense of power when the adrenaline is pumping. When they shout, pound, and spit out angry words, they actually think they are getting some respect, that others will listen, and that they are in charge and doing something that will benefit themselves. The opposite is actually true.

People who do not handle conflict well are those who:

- grew up in a home where conflict was denied or poorly handled
- believe that conflict is dangerous
- deny individual differences
- keep a relationship superficial to avoid conflict
- feel unsafe or ill at ease during conflict
- talk too much and listen too little because they feel insecure during conflict
- strive to "win" rather than resolve a conflict
- regularly feel misunderstood and disrespected during conflict
- hide their true feelings and bottle them

People who handle conflict well are those who:

- are open, honest, and have a strong commitment to resolving conflict
- respect themselves and their partner
- are aware of, expect, and welcome differences
- appreciate the uniqueness and differences of the other
- possess a strong sense of comfort and trust in the relationship
- do not ignore conflict
- can admit when wrong
- are not defensive or competitive with their partner
- congratulate themselves and their partner when differences are resolved happily

Clinical experience and research suggest that it is a person's parental background—especially the relationship with his mother—that predicts how successful he will be in marriage.[1] Beware of marrying anyone with parents who never fought or who fought violently. It is highly likely that your loved one has learned and uses a similar conflict-resolution style. In either case, he has learned all the wrong ways to handle a critical part of a relationship.

Danger Signal 2: Heavy Physical Involvement

Ed and Margie are both adult singles who have been previously married. They struck up a friendship at a function for Christian singles. Although each claims to be a committed Christian and feels somewhat guilty about it, they are having an intense sexual affair. Discussion about stopping the sexual portion of their relationship gets stymied. Most of their time together revolves around their sexual relationship. Their date life includes little verbal communication and few participation activities. Margie wishes there were more depth to their relationship but she is afraid of losing Ed. When a couple gets this involved physically, the other areas of their relationship fail to grow.

> *At one time, the Open University of Washington, D.C., offered a course on kissing. The course included instruction on the "Air Kiss," the "Dart and Dodge Kiss," and the "Inhalation Kiss."*
>
> Curious Facts

A good question to ask yourself is: If you took away the physical aspect of your relationship would your partner stick around? If not, you know what he or she wants. When you say no to physical intimacies does your partner respect and support your request? Is it easier to be sexually intimate than conversationally intimate? When a couple is not married, and sex or other heavy physical intimacies dominate the relationship, it is time to break up and begin fresh with someone else to achieve a balance in the emotional, physical, and spiritual development of a relationship.

Danger Signal 3: Conflicting Goals and Values

Phil and Pat think they are compatible since both enjoy skiing, country music, bird watching, and pizza. But this is only what they enjoy doing in their spare time. Actually their goals and values are very different. Phil is working his way through college so that he can become a social worker. He dreams of helping kids in the inner city. Pat isn't that interested in a profession. She wants to get married, work part time, and join a country club. She has visions of spending her days swimming and playing tennis.

Goals and values are what you are, who you are, and the beliefs you will hold for all the years to come. If one person

86

in a couple values home and family along with a simple life in the country and the other pursues status and materialism that a fast city life offers, their values contrast so sharply that no amount of compromise is likely to solve the differences. If one is deeply committed to God and the other is not, if one desires to serve humankind in a mission field and the other wants to make a million dollars in business, their values and goals are so different that no amount of compromise or prayer can help them solve the multitude of problems they will encounter.

It is very important to discuss and understand each other's current and long-term goals and values. Some couples attempt to set aside conflicting ideals saying that it doesn't matter. It will work out in time. But different goals and values can drive a couple apart. In a survey I conducted, college students indicated that disagreements over values and philosophy of life were the main sources of most conflicts in their love lives.

Danger Signal 4: Abuse

Marie was shaking violently while she sobbingly told her story. At seventeen she married her childhood sweetheart. Mac was the only fellow she had ever dated seriously, the only one she ever loved. She married him despite the fact that he was abusive. They had been dating for only three months when he became so angry with her that he hit her.

He had apologized immediately and said it would never happen again. Marie forgave him and their relationship continued—and so did the physical abuse whenever his temper flared. Profuse apologies always followed, and Marie always forgave him. Marie didn't like this part of their relationship, but Mac was so wonderful when he wasn't abusing her, she married him. When she was five months pregnant, he became angry again and pounded on her abdomen, killing the child. Mac is now serving a prison term for murder, and

Marie is dealing with the psychological aftermath of her trauma.

One study revealed that one in ten teens experiences physical violence in a dating relationship (slapping, hitting, or punching). National statistics show that about 12 percent of high school students experience violence in a dating relationship before graduating. The likelihood of violence increases to 20–25 percent by the time they are in college. A St. Louis study of 885 teenagers showed that 33 percent had been threatened by physical violence in dating relationships.[2]

Some abuse is emotional. A person can play any number of "mind games" that relegate his loved one to the land of the stupid. The St. Louis study showed that 52 percent of the subjects had experienced one or more of the following forms of emotional abuse in their dating relationships: constant criticism, blame for all problems, threats of physical harm, isolation, repeated insults, destruction of possessions, and being completely ignored.[3] Intentional public humiliation that makes someone look and feel like a fool in front of others is also a form of emotional abuse.

Red flags should go up any time you are put down. If your date makes remarks about how dumb, clumsy, or stupid you are, if he criticizes the way you dress or behave, you can be sure that more criticism will follow. This is not healthy. Healthy relationships affirm your worth and make you feel better about yourself.

Make it clear early in a relationship that you will not tolerate put-downs or negative remarks. If your partner refuses to stop, get out of the relationship before your self-worth is destroyed.

To tolerate emotional or physical abuse while suffering in silence, hoping the other person will change his behavior, only encourages such behavior and is degrading to your self-worth. Anytime a relationship includes any degree of abuse, get out! Things won't improve. To continue in a relationship of this nature shows gross insecurity and a lack of self-esteem. Anyone with positive feelings of worth would not allow herself to be used as a punching bag or the butt of jokes. There is never a good excuse for causing physical or emotional pain. End it!

Look for clues, such as threats, repeated insults or criticism, and destruction of possessions, to help you determine whether you are in a potentially abusive relationship. Rarely does abuse surface on the first date. These clues will help you determine whether your relationship will remain healthy.

If either of you is from a family in which there was emotional abuse or violence—child abuse, wife beating—*proceed with caution* because a child is prone to follow in the footsteps of his parents. It is something that should be discussed as the intimacy and trust levels of your relationship increase. Discuss how the victim or witness of the abuse has learned to cope, how it affects that person today, and if professional help has been sought to overcome the trauma.

Danger Signal 5: Lack of Spiritual Oneness

A couple who are desperately in love get very uncomfortable when someone questions their spiritual oneness, quoting Paul's famous passage:

> Do not be yoked together with unbelievers. For what do righteousness and wickedness have in common? Or what fellowship can light have with darkness? What harmony is there between Christ and Belial? What does a believer have in common with an unbeliever?
>
> 2 Corinthians 6:14–15

This is when people begin to rationalize: He's not a Christian but he goes to church with me and I just know he's going to convert . . . But there's no one at church to date. What do you want me to do? Become a monk? . . . He's not a Christian but he has higher moral standards than all the other men I've dated. It's amazing how much disobedience flourishes under rationalization.

I know and understand the complaints. Looking for someone with whom you can share spiritual oneness drastically reduces the field of eligible candidates. There *is* a chance that a person may convert . . . sometime. But the admonition against a relationship between a believer and an unbeliever still exists. So instead of trying to ignore the problem, justify the relationship, or disobey, you must take a hard look at what this means for you and the one you love. If you don't do it now, you will later have to deal with the consequences of having a spiritually incompatible spouse.

I was raised in such a home. My mother was a committed Christian and my father practiced no religion. When my parents were first married, my dad went to church with my mother out of courtesy. My sister and I were educated in my mother's faith without disapproval from my father. In spite of these concessions, there was a host of things my mother and father never shared. There were never any discussions about what they had learned through personal Bible study. Mother could not share with him any answers to prayer. There was no trading of information and insights found through reading Christian books and articles. There were no long walks where they discussed what God could do through them as a witnessing team or when they sought His will. There was no encouragement for committing their lives to God and no open talk about sin and striving toward greater obedience.

My mother went to church alone—for twenty-five years. Then my father's life was snuffed out prematurely by a massive heart attack allowing him no time to make a decision for Christ. After his death, my mother wistfully shared her hurt with me, "As happy as your father and I were, if I had it to do over again, I would not marry him."

I was shocked. "Why?" I asked.

"There was no spiritual oneness," she explained. "Going to church alone all those years and carrying alone the burden for the spiritual development of you girls was painful. A lifetime without sharing on a spiritual level is too much."

There are scores of Christ-like men and women in our churches just like my mother—married to unbelievers. Some of them became Christians after they married. Others married without heeding scriptural advice. But they all carry the pain of spiritual loneliness. God gave us this command to help us avoid such pain.

Imagine the frustration of two builders trying to work on the same home from two different sets of building plans. Conflicting measurements, designs, and materials would produce such conflict and confusion that the project would be futile. Even a casual observer would say, "You can't build a house from two separate blueprints."

The same advice goes for naive lovers who enter marriage with differing sets of spiritual blueprints. If one is a Christian and the other is not, they have entered an arena where oneness will never be achieved. All the seminars, books, counseling, and tears cannot solve the problems this couple will encounter. Likewise a Spirit-filled Christian should never settle for a nominal churchgoer who does little more than show up for church when convenient or one who leads a double life—pious at church and devilish at home.

One reason spiritual compatibility is so important is that during a time of stress, both can tap into a source of strength to carry them through adversity. No couple goes through life without being touched by adversity or tragedy. This imperfect world carries much evil, heartache, pain, disappointment, illness, emotional upheavals, financial setbacks, and death. What a difference it makes in marriage when both partners can turn to God in the midst of turmoil and together find a refuge and strength, a present help in time of need.

Another reason God insists on spiritual compatibility is so children can be raised by parents who share a common faith. More than any other time in history, children need parents who can point the way to Jesus, parents who present a united front spiritually. Then it will be easier for children to adopt the same value system and to establish their own strong faith.

"Do not be yoked together with unbelievers" is godly wisdom. Every unmarried Christian must heed it. This advice isn't given to keep you from finding a mate, but to protect you from unknown future pain. Yet there are some of you who are so desperately in love, so wrapped up romantically with someone who doesn't share your faith, that you cannot bear the thought of a future without that person. What happens now? I do not reply lightly. My counsel is based on God's Word, personal experience from observing my parents, and a quarter of a century in dealing with family life education. I recommend the relationship be ended.

If you are currently in a romantic relationship with someone who does not share your spiritual values, you need courage to end it. You must get out, call it off, and make a clean break. The pain will be oppressive, but the peace afterward will be even more incredible. Surround yourself with Christian friends who can support you in prayer. If you choose to disobey this admonition, you are headed for certain disaster and a lonely future. If you make the hard choice now, you will have peace later on.

So many times during our life together my husband, Harry, and I have faced tough decisions. We seek God's direction together and separately—about everything: sacrificial giving, country living as opposed to city living, God's call to begin a ministry. Each time we seek God's direction, He leads the two of us to similar conclusions. This is being equally yoked. This is true spiritual compatibility.

Danger Signal 6: Separation

Rita and George met at an annual singles convention sponsored by their church at a national park. The friendship that was initially sparked there led to romance—via phone and mail. Rita lived in Arizona and George in Missouri. This couple married after two years. Four years later they were divorced. In questioning them about the building of their relationship, I learned that in their two-year romance they had only seen each other twice a month.

Even though Rita and George believed they knew each other and had followed my rule—waiting at least two years before marrying—their relationship failed. Why? This couple had had a relationship for two years but they did not know each other because they had not had enough face-to-face interaction. Fifty-five percent of communication is delivered through posture, facial expressions, and gestures. When talking to someone on the phone, you have the 38 percent of the message that is tone of voice and the 7 percent verbal message that you can tap to get to know someone. But a whopping 55 percent of the message (the nonverbals) isn't there. In letters, where only 7 percent of the message comes through, 93 percent of the message is missing.

> _A Taiwanese man once wrote seven hundred love letters to a woman over the course of two years. The letters worked: The woman married the postman who delivered all the letters._
>
> True Remarkable Occurrences

All the long-distance phone calls, love letters, and promises can't stall the mortality rate on long-distance romance. A couple separated by distance must either arrange to get together more frequently to test their relationship or go together for a longer period of time.

Danger Signal 7: A BTN

Any relationship that's okay, but not great, is BTN—better than nothing.[4] A BTN is a "nice" relationship with the wrong person. BTNs are all those people you have cared about in the past but who never cared about you or ones that cared about you but in whom you weren't that interested. These relationships are only partially satisfying but drag on and on. BTNs are okay if you recognize that they are BTNs and that's all you want. But if you are looking for a lifelong commitment, then BTNs take you out of circulation and consume time and energy that should be available for a new relationship.

BTNs waste precious time, yet people stay in them because of the security they offer. They are safe relationships even if they aren't wonderful. They also meet short-term intimacy needs, although they thwart long-term goals. Often people don't know how to get out of a BTN. It's been going on for so long that it's painful to think of ending it. In other words, people stay in BTNs long after they should because they didn't have what it takes to get out early enough in the relationship when it would have been infinitely easier.

Some people stay in BTNs because these relationships seem better than nothing, but in reality they are worse than nothing. They chip away at your self-esteem. Your love relationship must be reinforced by positive messages. Whenever you spend time with a person who does not contribute to your self-esteem, you will have a difficult time feeling good about yourself. The very fact that you are willing to stay in a BTN relationship says that your self-esteem is already in trouble. If you are in a relationship that does not help you feel good about yourself, but instead eats away at your feelings of self-worth, it becomes critical to end it.

If a relationship isn't working, even though parts of it may be great, it is much better to get out when you first realize the problems. That moment may come on your first date or it may come five months later.

Some cases are more clear-cut than others. If you become involved with someone and learn he is married, end it. If you fall in love with someone and find out he is a homosexual, don't hang around to see if you can "fix" him. The same goes if you learn about drug or alcohol addiction or a history of violence or sexual abuse.

If you want to be part of a forever relationship and the one you are in isn't going in that direction, the earlier you say no the better it will be for you.

6

Ending It

He's been treating you differently. You can't quite put your finger on what it is, but things just aren't the same. Last night he declined to come in after your date. He said he needed to get home. His goodnight kisses indicate he has something else on his mind. Lately you phone him more than he calls you.

He doesn't seem to be as happy as he used to be. He doesn't laugh and joke and share as much as he once did. When you ask him if there is anything wrong, he always says no. But nagging doubts plague you. Then panic begins to rise. You don't hear from him for several days and you don't call him either. When you finally see him again, you hardly dare ask, "What's the matter between us?"

He looks away. His shoulders droop. You're afraid to hear the answer: "I guess it's time to call this off."

It's over. The one you love doesn't love you anymore and wants to move on. What happens now? You may never have thought of it this way, but dating forms a cycle—dating around, steady dating, breaking up; dating around, steady dating, breaking up; et cetera. Until you marry, you will break up again and again.

A major national survey was conducted on single adults (ages twenty to fifty-five) and the results were published in the book _Singles: The New Americans._[1] One question asked was, "What is the most frequent reason you stop dating someone?" The responses were as follows:

	Men	Women
I find him/her dull and superficial.	30%	34%
(For men) She refuses to have sex.	6	
(For women) All he wants is sex.		13
He/she is immature or neurotic.	20	18
He/she is a poor lover.	3	3
It's usually my way to go out with a man/woman a few times and then move on.	15	8
(For men) She presses me too quickly for intimacy.	10	
(For women) He shows no signs of serious interest or involvement.		13
She loses interest./He stops calling.	12	7
Don't know.	5	6

Ending It Like a Klutz

Much of the pain associated with breaking up could be avoided if a little tact were used during the process. The following are some hurtful and un-Christian ways of ending it that should be avoided like the plague:

Sporting a new friend on your arm to transmit the "It's over" message. This is the cruelest method of getting the news across.

Disappearing without a word. Failing to call or meet as you usually do isn't the way to go either. This causes your partner to guess what happened: Maybe I've said or done something to hurt her feelings; or, He's probably been trying to ditch me for weeks.

Telling your partner off. Fran was bored with Larry and had found someone else to whom she was attracted. Fran detests confrontations, so she magnified Larry's negative traits in her mind so she could justify "telling him off." The next time Larry did something that displeased her she let him have it. Now Larry is very hurt. Not only has Fran dumped him, but she has also made him feel like an unworthy and unlikable person.

The hot-and-cold treatment. Bruce is seriously thinking about breaking up with Lori. He's tired of her yet he needs the security of their relationship. Besides, Lori is good-looking, and the guys envy his relationship with her. He vacillates in his treatment of her according to his current mood—sometimes he is thoughtful and attentive; other times he treats her coldly. By treating her attentively, he is trying to convince himself that they can still make a go of it. By ignoring her he is signaling that it is all over. Such treatment is very confusing to the other person. Don't indulge in it while you try to make up your mind.

Breaking up at the wrong time or place. Avoid breaking up during the holidays or just before the major social event of the year. This makes a difficult situation even harder. Never break up in front of others or in a public place. The breaking of a relationship between two people who once cared for each other is a private affair. It would be best to go to a private, unfamiliar, unromantic place to tell the other your feelings. Don't go to your favorite spot or the place where you met.

If you are separated by distance you may have to resort to a Dear John or Dear Jane letter. This type of letter has become the butt of many jokes, but in reality expressing yourself in writing clarifies your thinking and will help you express yourself clearly. However, if possible, it is always best to end a relationship face-to-face. After delivering the message, allow time to talk it over. Don't just say it and run. If you've been special friends you owe it to the other to stick around long enough to answer questions and try to ease the pain. Treat the other person as you would want to be treated.

Sending messages that could be misinterpreted. If you feel the time has come to break your relationship, examine your reasons carefully and then state them openly, clearly, and honestly. Be careful to say what you mean. You may want to soften the blow of the breakup but you must do it in such a way that your message won't be misunderstood. Don't leave the other person hanging or with hope that you may change your mind or something might change. Be definite.

An immature person will choose the easy way out of a relationship and move on to a new partner while leaving the other hurting and wondering why. This immature person will likely blame the other rather than accept her share of responsibility for the failure of the relationship. A mature person faces inadequacies in a relationship and thoughtfully evaluates whether they can be overcome or whether she and her partner should separate.

An immature person may end a relationship just because the other individual no longer meets her needs. How selfish it is to view a relationship only in terms of having one's own personal needs met. Such an immature individual has failed to see that she too has a responsibility for certain aspects of the relationship.

> *In Connecticut in the 1950s, some girls wore "obit bracelets." When a girl broke up with a boy, she added his initials to the bracelet.*
>
> From Front Porch to Back Seat

99

A mature individual does all she can to make a relationship work. If that's impossible, the mature person ends it in a caring way so that bitterness does not develop between them. This is possible when the couple concentrate on the positives: the good things the two have shared, the pleasant memories of good times, and the personal growth that resulted from the friendship.

Ending It with Class

For a couple who have cared about each other there is no easy way to break up. There is a high probability that there will be hurt feelings, disappointment, and pain. But it *is* possible to soften the blow and prevent further complications. Here are some suggestions.

Pray about It

Ask the Lord to make it clear that you have chosen the right course of action. Request divine guidance as you carry out your decision with kindness. The Bible says:

> "For I know the plans I have for you," declares the LORD, "plans to prosper you and not to harm you, plans to give you hope and a future. Then you will call upon me and come and pray to me, and I will listen to you. You will seek me and find me when you seek me with all your heart. I will be found by you."
>
> Jeremiah 29:11–14

He will not only guide you but also give you strength to do what is right. Ask God to give you the right words to speak and to help you deliver them as kindly as possible under the circumstances. Pray that the person you are breaking off with will get over the breakup without suffering serious emotional or physical problems.

Seek Advice

If you have doubts about your decision to call it quits, seek advice from someone you trust and respect. When we are emotionally upset, we often say and do things we regret later. Many couples who have broken up during the heat of an argument later wish they hadn't. Unburden yourself, if necessary, to a trusted friend, a minister, or a counselor. Explaining the whole situation in detail will help clear your mind, and the objective opinion of someone not emotionally involved often proves helpful.

A Three-Step Plan

Beth thinks Matt is too involved with sports and she resents attending three games a week during baseball, basketball, and football seasons. Matt says that sports are very important to him and Beth better get used to it. Beth's feelings get hurt. Matt loses his temper and Beth cries. Each says a few more hurtful things and they each go their separate ways. Their last memory of each other is bitter. Each has his or her pride at stake and they both protect themselves by remaining enemies. The hurt lingers for months, which keeps them from freely moving into new relationships. And their friendship is lost forever.

It doesn't have to be this way. Even though breaking up will always hurt, there are less painful ways to end relationships. This three-step plan is a winner:

1. *Point out something good about the other person.* When you break up with your partner, he feels unloved and rejected and it is a major loss to his self-image. So avoid dragging up all the negatives about the other person. Instead, emphasize all the good times you have had together. Mention at least one way in which the other person has contributed to your relationship and spell out your appreciation for the finer qualities you have admired.

Instead of letting the relationship end in bitterness, Beth could have said, "Matt, I like you. We've had some great times together. You've taught me a lot about life, men, and relationships. I'll always remember the fun we had at the singles retreat."

2. *Admit your own failures.* It takes two to make a relationship and both make mistakes. In Beth and Matt's relationship, Beth is partly to blame for the failure. Admitting this takes maturity but will provide insight for Beth and soften the blow for Matt.

"I can see now that I've been making you unhappy by not supporting your love for sports. I pretended to enjoy them as much as you did, at least at first. I wasn't being honest. I never meant to hurt you. I'm sorry for this."

3. *Give an honest reason for the breakup.* You have a responsibility to tell the other person why you want to break up. Everyone I've ever talked to wants to know the reason even though it may hurt to find out. In the long run it will prove beneficial. Mature people want to learn from their mistakes. So honestly and openly state the problem without being brutally frank. Do not deliver negative information unless you can do it kindly.

"Matt, I need more from this relationship than I'm getting. Sports bore me and I need someone who can share my love for concerts and the arts. I think it better that we build a relationship with someone who shares our passion for the things we love. I will fondly remember the good times we have shared and I want to consider you a friend for life."

It still hurts. It is worse for Matt than for Beth since he is the one being rejected. But this is better than angry words and bitter feelings that can linger for months, even years.

Sometimes, when the emotional dependence on the relationship has been great, the one who wants the relationship to continue may use threats, blackmail, or even violence to get his way. There may be threats to tell personal secrets, to get high or drunk, or to commit suicide. These wild threats are usually only desperate attempts to hold on. But don't count on it. Suicide threats should be taken seriously. Immediately report such threats to a counselor or your pastor. This is proof that the person is not emotionally stable. Under no circumstances should you stay in a relationship just to pacify threats of suicide, violence, or blackmail.

Letting Go

It's over. The one you love wants out. What will you do?

Yes	No	
		1. Will you fall on your knees and beg him or her to take you back?
		2. Will you make wild promises to change and become exactly what the person wants you to be?
		3. Will you cry uncontrollably so he or she will feel sorry for you? If that doesn't work, you'll beg and cry some more, allowing deep sobs to rack your body.
		4. Will you threaten suicide?
		5. Will you thank him or her for the good times you have shared and leave with your head high and your self-worth intact? (Then fall apart privately if you feel you must.)

If you have never been through the trauma of a broken romance, chances are that someday you will. How you cope with it when it happens tells a lot about you. There are dignified ways to survive. If you can handle a breakup with a little class, it will do wonders for your self-esteem and help you save face.

ihailo Tolotos never had the heartbreaking experience of breaking up with a girl. That's because this Greek monk, who died in 1938 at the age of eighty-two, never looked at a female during his entire life.

The day after he was born, Mihailo's mother died and he was taken to a monastery high in the mountains. Because female wildlife were not allowed in the monastery, Mihailo never even saw a female animal his entire life.

Incredible!

You may be so hurt that you want to angrily lash out at the one who has hurt you. The temptation to do so usually is an attempt to justify the hurt. You may also be tempted to rant and rave about how stupid he is anyway and how you should have broken it off ages ago. But refuse to mend your broken ego by slandering the other person. Try not to defend yourself by intimating, You're the bad guy. I'm the good guy. Or, When word gets around what you're really like, buddy, no one will want you either! I'll see to it that you get what's coming to you! Forget about saying, "If I can't have you, I will personally see to it that no one else will want you either!" You may have these thoughts but don't verbalize them. Keep to yourself any personal problems the two of you have had. Avoid the desire to broadcast information and gossip to your friends. The nicest thing you can say (for yourself and the other person) is: "We used to go together, and he is a fine person. We'll always be friends." If you circulate damaging information, you do yourself a serious disservice. If the other person was such a jerk or bimbo, why did you go with him anyway? Don't advertise your own poor judgment!

You may be tempted, when one romance has ended, to rush into an intense relationship with someone new, partly for revenge and partly to prove how desirable you are. Resist the temptation! It is likely that you are too emotionally raw to handle it. So if you cry on Ron's shoulder because you and Fred have broken up, it is all right to accept Ron's sympathy but don't get carried away. Remember that you are very vulnerable to any attention right now and your inclination will be to leap at any chance to fill the void in your life. Rebound romances are phony to the core. Time and healing are needed before you will be ready to build a love relationship with anyone. At any cost, avoid marriage on the rebound. These marriages have little chance of succeeding because they usually aren't based on long acquaintance, matched backgrounds, shared values, and maturity. Your pride may hit rock bottom following a breakup but marrying someone on the rebound will only intensify an already traumatic situation.

Keys to Survival

Surviving a breakup can be difficult, particularly if you still care for the person. But how much better to leave the other person wondering if a terrible mistake has been made in breaking up with you than creating a scene and removing all doubt. Try to leave the other person thinking, "She is really something," rather than, "Whew! Am I ever glad to be rid of that one!"

Here are some tips to lessen the pain:

1. _Talk it over with your dating partner._ The breakup may have come as a surprise or shock. You may not understand what happened, why it is over. You have every right to ask your partner about it if you have not been told. You may also say, if you care to, that it will be difficult to stop loving him. Talk it over as much as you need to and the other person is willing. But when all is said and done, accept the situation and use it to your advantage rather than detriment. Instead of looking and acting like your world has fallen apart, bow out gracefully. Carry your self-respect away with you.

2. Go ahead and cry about it if you need to. Tears are a normal reaction during a time of hurt. If you feel like crying about it, go ahead—and this advice goes for males as well as for females. Crying is a natural release for stressful situations and a healthy release for pressures that build up. Just do your weeping privately.

Where Do You Go from Here?

Okay. The relationship has ended. Your entire life seems empty, off kilter, and out of whack. You feel like quitting your job, getting drunk, running away, jumping off a cliff, or dropping out of the human race. You may feel lower than ever before. What now? Even if you do get over a breakup with a minimum amount of pain, there are still some questions to answer. "What will I do now?" comes first. Getting back into circulation takes time and effort.

Give yourself a chance to heal. Although some people take longer to recuperate than others, time is a wonderful healer. The time involved in bouncing back from heartbreak will be in direct proportion to the intensity of the severed relationship, the length of time you went together, and whether you were sexually involved.

While you are recovering, take time to look at yourself and evaluate your progress in personal growth. After you have sorted out your responsibility for what happened and talked it over with a friend, get on with life. Remember, just because someone has broken off with you does not mean that no one in the world wants you or that you are not a worthy person. You may be tempted to bask in your own misery and pain while trying to enlist the sympathy of friends. But a better course of action is to put the past behind you and leave it there. Dwelling on the past will only lead to self-pity and depression. Pity parties are lonely affairs.

Instead, keep yourself busy. Rather than hibernating and brooding over your failures, enter group activities that will distract your mind from your problems. Take up a new hobby, attend a night class, volunteer to work with teens at your church, or do something special for a friend. This way you will be more inclined to forget your own troubles as you think of others who just may have bigger problems than you.

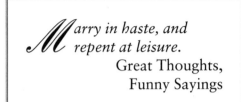

Marry in haste, and repent at leisure.
Great Thoughts,
Funny Sayings

And pray about it. God knows and cares about what has happened to you. Tell him how you hurt, and ask Him to help you heal. Claim the promise that "in all things God works for the good of those who love him" (Rom. 8:28). God has a purpose in allowing hurt to touch our lives. It teaches us to respond by seeking a closer walk with God. Whatever the reason hurt enters your life, you must trust God.

Andraé Crouch, the gospel singer, loved a woman ardently. Then one day they broke up. Andraé Crouch hurt deeply but he turned his thoughts to God, and out of the depths of his grief he wrote the beautiful gospel song "Through It All." You may never have thought of the song as a breakup song, but it is. Through it all Andraé Crouch came to depend on God's Word. Through it all he learned that God could indeed solve his problems.

Full Recovery

Don't be surprised if full recovery from the pain of a breakup takes time. Psychologists have discovered that people go through fixed stages following intense grief. This process applies regardless of the kind of loss—death of a loved one, divorce, or the breakup of a serious relationship.

The breaking up process goes through four distinct stages, which take approximately two years. The interesting thing

107

is these stages are unavoidable. You can delay going through the stages, but to become whole again you will need to proceed through all four.[2]

Stage 1: Feeling terrible loss. This stage lasts anywhere from two weeks to two months. When you have truly loved someone, the breaking up process will be like a part of you is being cut off. Even if you want to be rid of this person, you will still pass through this stage. The longer you have gone together, the longer this stage will last. Typical reactions during this stage will include:

- deep sadness
- feeling hopeless
- no appetite
- immersion in painful memories
- feeling sorry for self
- difficulty getting through each day

To get through stage 1 you need to get the pain out by crying as much as possible. Holding it in will only delay the stage. Spend time with family and friends, avoiding evenings and weekends when you sit alone with nothing to do. Take good care of your health during this phase, eating regularly even when you don't feel like it. A good exercise program would also help with emotional stability.

Stage 2: Adjustment. The most acute phase is over and you will notice that from time to time you begin to feel a little better. You no longer feel the intense pain. You begin to get your life back on track and become interested again in the opposite sex. This phase usually lasts two to six months and you will find that you can:

- consider life bearable
- talk about your former partner without falling apart
- be interested in the opposite sex

- begin making plans for the future
- begin enjoying life again
- experience only occasional intense grief (one to two times a week)
- more clearly see what went wrong

Stage 3: Healing. Stage 3 usually takes six months to one year. During this phase you begin to feel normal again on a daily basis. You may become interested in beginning a new relationship. The wounds are healing. You have survived. During this phase you will notice that you:

- have interest in a new relationship
- look and feel better
- have hope for the future
- feel sad only once every week or two

Stage 4: Recovery. Stage 4 is a transitional stage. It can take from one to two years. The fresh pain of the breakup is behind you and you have surrounded yourself with new friends, new activities, and new interests. You are emotionally healthy enough to risk loving again.

Risking It Again

The natural inclination after hurt is to insulate yourself so no one can ever hurt you again. Some protection may be necessary during the healing process, but a time comes when it is necessary to risk a new relationship. Withdrawing into a cocoon cuts you off from building new friendships.

The greatest hazard in life is to risk nothing. In risking nothing you may avoid some future hurt, but you cannot grow, change, learn to live, or relate better with others. No one is chained to the heartbreak of a broken romance. Peace comes as you let go of the hurt and risk loving again.

The End Goal

After you have invested time, effort, and caring into a relationship, it is sad to lose the person as a friend just because the romance is over. When appropriate, attempt to reestablish a friendship with your ex-partner. This isn't always possible but should be the ultimate goal. A period of time will be needed for healing. If you attempt too soon to reestablish the friendship after a breakup, it might be interpreted as an effort to revive the romance. So give it time and space. Then work at staying or becoming friends.

Dave and Lisa dated for a year before their romance died a natural death. Since both attended the same church, they were often together during church activities. At first they avoided each other. But eventually, when the initial hurt died, they became friends again. One day Lisa bought a new car right off the showroom floor and just had to share her joy with a friend. The first person who got a ride in her new car was Dave. After all, he was one of her best friends!

It's worth the effort, whenever possible, to stay friends. As Charlie Brown says, "I need all the friends I can get." We all do.

Part 4
True Love
and Infatuation

7

True Love

How to Recognize the Real Thing
When It Comes Along

Some things remain constant no matter how much the world changes. One of those constants is the desire to love and be loved. We all need that feeling of belonging and caring that is the result of being "in love." In return, there is nothing that produces more happiness and security than the assurance that someone cares deeply about you.

The need to love and be loved is at the very core of our being. The search for intimacy to fill this need is deep-seated. It begins when we are born and never ends.

Falling in love is one of the most exciting events in a person's life. Everyone wants to find true love, and when it happens, life takes on new meaning. Sudden energy surges through the system. A new enthusiasm for living provides a zest for even routine tasks. A special chemistry works overtime. Time is too short when two people in love are together and too long when they are apart.

In the early stages of love, time together is filled with exciting adventures and affectionate interludes. Each look and

113

touch, every kiss and conversation takes on monumental proportions. Everything is so right, so good, so perfect. Then, as the weeks slip by, everyone faces the same challenging question, "How do I know if this is the real thing?" You have probably asked this question or a similar one:

- I'm in a good relationship with someone I really care about. Everything between us is good. No problems. But how can I tell if what we have is the real thing?
- I'm just out of a very painful relationship. I'm putting my life together again but I never want to go through what I have just been through. Is there any way to tell in advance if I have found the "real thing"?
- I've been in one relationship after another and never seem to find the "real thing." Where and how do I find lasting love? I'm desperate to find true love before it's too late!

The frustration expressed by these people is understandable; falling in love at seventeen is very different from falling in love at thirty-seven or fifty-seven. A seventeen-year-old is likely to fall in love with the first attractive available person, convinced that this is "the one." A teenager rushes into what he believes is the perfect relationship. When the relationship fails, he hurries into the next one. This pattern is likely repeated over and over without much thought being given to how love works, the dynamics of sustaining love, or what love is and isn't.

The mature adult is more concerned than the teenager about developing a lasting relationship. As he grows older, however, the pool of available partners becomes smaller.

None of us deliberately sets out to make wrong choices in our love life. We want our relationships to work. At the time we make our decision about who is right for us, we believe with all our heart that we are making the right choice. More often than we like to admit, that choice is wrong. Too late we ask ourself:

- Why couldn't I see what she was really like sooner?
- She was so wonderful at first. Now I can't stand anything about her! Who changed? Her or me?
- This time I was so sure that I'd found the right person. How can something that seems so right turn so sour?

> *P*sychologists at an international confer-ence on Love and Attraction defined love as "the cogni-tive-affective state character-ized by intrusive and obses-sive fantasizing concerning reciprocity of amorant feel-ings by the object of the amorance." Now that's help-ful information!
>
> Curious Facts

As mature adults, we be-lieve we should be able to discern true love. But the feel-ings we had at seventeen are just as likely to color and con-fuse judgment in later years as earlier years. Sometimes, because we haven't experienced the exhilaration in so many years, the excitement overpowers good sense.

Adult singles in their romantic relationships experience many of the same feelings so evident in teen dating—the exhilaration, quickened sexual response, rush of excitement, urgency of diminished time—all amplified with age since time for them is running out. For example, a woman approaching the age of forty realizes her biological clock is running down. What this means then, as Dr. James Dobson states, is "grownups still love the thrill of the chase, the lure of the unattainable, the excitement of the new and boredom with the old."[1]

An old adage states that men love women in proportion to their strangeness to them, and even as adults this continues to ring true. Genuine love will, of course, temper these immature impulses, but they will still remain evident. Love is so exhila-rating that some people deliberately close their eyes to anything that might mar the experience. Differentiating between true love and adolescent love is complicated, but applying the "test of time"—two full years of dating before marriage—will help.

To clarify what you really know about "true love" take the True Love Test below. Then read the chapter to clarify issues where you disagree or are confused.

True Love Test

Circle the letter that identifies your present belief. (Answers are given on page 134.)

True	*False*	*Unsure*	
T	F	U	1. Men fall in love more rapidly than women.
T	F	U	2. It is easier for adults to determine if they've found true love than it is for teenagers.
T	F	U	3. When you find true love, you will know it is the real thing.
T	F	U	4. When you find true love, you should marry as soon as possible.
T	F	U	5. Infatuation and true love are so different that it is easy to tell one from the other.
T	F	U	6. Sexual attraction can be as urgent in true love as in infatuation.
T	F	U	7. When a woman falls in love, she is more emotional and romantic than a man.
T	F	U	8. One of the best ways to find true love is to first be friends with a person for a long time.
T	F	U	9. True love usually develops rapidly and intensely.
T	F	U	10. If you and your partner are truly in love, you will never argue.

True	False	Unsure	
T	F	U	11. It is possible to be in love with more than one person at a time.
T	F	U	12. A strong sexual attraction is an indication of true love.
T	F	U	13. Having the approval of family and friends for your marriage is one of the most important factors in determining future happiness.
T	F	U	14. Early in a relationship most people are open and honest about their faults and inadequacies.
T	F	U	15. It is possible for a couple to determine true love after careful observation of each other for a few months.
T	F	U	16. Love at first sight is possible for mature adults.
T	F	U	17. Sex prior to marriage is acceptable after a couple becomes engaged.
T	F	U	18. Due to maturity and life experience, older adults need less pastoral counseling prior to marriage than do young adults.
T	F	U	19. When you find the right person and true love, all obstacles can be overcome through patience and prayer.
T	F	U	20. God has created and chosen one special person for you and through prayer and searching you will be guided to this person.

True Love Conquers All

Many singles are doomed before they begin building a relationship because they have bought into the theory that true love conquers all: "Regardless of what the problem is, we can beat it." "We love each other so much we can make our relationship work." "No problem is too big for our love."

Anyone who buys into this theory is not facing reality. Couples with one or more of the following problems may hold to the love-conquers-all theory:

- vast age differences
- racial or cultural differences
- multiple marriages by one or both partners
- inability to express feelings
- not getting along with the other's children
- differences in religious background
- wanting or not wanting children

Tina and Max, who were both in their early thirties, had been dating for a year. Tina was brought up in a strict religious home and Max was brought up in a home totally devoid of religion. Before meeting Tina, he had never even been to church. They had discussed their religious differences from time to time, but not in depth. Max went to church with Tina to make her happy but had never made a commitment to the Lord. Because he attended church with her most of the time, Tina thought Max was accepting her religion even though Max never said anything to lead her to this conclusion. Both skirted the issue because they got along so well in other ways. Neither wanted to rock the boat. Inwardly Tina knew she could never give up her faith, and Max knew he couldn't ever be religious like Tina. At first, both thought their love for each other could beat all obstacles.

Tina and Max really loved each other. But no matter how much they loved each other, neither could ever be happy with life or with themselves unless they remained true to their own beliefs, regardless of how much they cared for each other. By skirting the issue of religious differences, they were really saying to each other, "If we really love each other enough, we can overcome this problem. True love can conquer anything." So they kept trying longer and harder to love each other rather than facing the obvious. Their relationship was prolonged long after it should have ended.

Love Defined

It isn't easy to state with accuracy precisely what love is. George Bernard Shaw said that *love* was the most misused and misunderstood word in our vocabulary. I tend to agree. How would you define love? The following is a collection of love definitions.

Love is a state of perpetual anesthesia.

Love is a grave mental disease.

Love is a fiend, a fire, a heaven, a hell, where pleasure, pain, and sad repentance dwell.

Love is a folly of the mind, an unquenchable fire, a hunger without surfeit, a sweet delight, a pleasing madness, a labor without repose and a repose without labor.

Love is a feeling you feel when you feel you are going to get a feeling you never felt before.

Love is when two people are under the influence of the most violent, most insane, most delusive, and most transient of passions, and they are required to swear that they will remain in that excited, abnormal, and exhausting condition continuously until death do them part.

119

> To love somebody is not just a strong feeling—it is a deci-
> sion, it is a judgment, it is a promise.
> Love is an unconditional commitment to an imperfect
> person.

The term *love* is used in a great many different senses. We say for example: "I love my mother"; "I love God"; "I love my dog"; "I love ice cream." I assume you do not have the same emotional response for your dog that you do for God! The word is so overused that it has become trivialized.

So what is love? Instead of trying to reconcile all these definitions, some of which are serious, others hackneyed, let's get to a working definition. *True love is caring as much about your partner's future, welfare, hopes, and dreams as you do about your own.* And this commitment to care is made because of the pleasure your partner gives you. You are willing to make a commitment because you sense fulfillment as well as growth in your relationship. Love is that feeling of finally meeting someone who truly understands you, someone who provides a new sense of validation, someone who perceives life the way you do, a true soul mate. It's a wonderful feeling of bonding.

But it is difficult even for the best definition to convey the excitement, adventure, and pleasure that go with being in love. Love is a powerful force and although it does not exactly make the world go round, as the old saying asserts, it certainly is a life-changing, mind-boggling experience.

Setting the Stage—Learning to Love

Research points out that we are conditioned or pro-grammed, while we are growing up, to fall in love. How does such conditioning occur? First of all, a person must be raised in a family that believes in the concept of true love, teaches it, and lives by it. Second, the concept is reinforced by a culture that does likewise. And certainly all western cultures teach it to their young through a continuous parade of romantic adventures in the mass media. Both elements—home and society—teach young people to expect love, desire love, and seek love. This creates a mind-set that makes falling in love preferable to any other state of being. By the time children reach their teen years, they not only want to fall in love but are expected to do so.

By the time we are eighteen or nineteen years old most of us have been "in love" two or three times, researchers say. We seem to fall in and out of love as naturally as breathing. But if it is so natural, why do we make such a mess of it and fail at it with such regularity? The reason is we have never learned to love properly.

We _learn_ to love? Yes, the ability to love others is learned early in life through observation, imitation, and practice. When we enter into a love relationship with someone, we bring with us all the love lessons we have learned and practiced since birth. As infants our love lessons were completely one-sided. Our parents filled our needs for survival. We eventually began reaching out, responding to, and smiling at those special people who satisfied our needs. The bonds of attachment were formed long before the words "I love you" were understood.

We learned to love through parental example. The nurturing we received through tender touching, kind words, kissing, and caressing during childhood prepared us for adult relationships where lovers caress, kiss, and express their feelings of love for each other. Children who grow up in emotionally or physically abusive homes or in cold, forbidding homes, where emotional and physical warmth are withheld and where love is rarely expressed, will find it difficult if not impossible to establish a warm supportive love relationship as an adult.

Another way we learn to love is by observing the love our parents express to each other. When Mom and Dad are affec-

121

tionate, we learn that this is how husband and wife treat each other. When patterns of coldness, silence, anger, and withdrawal are noted, we learn that this is the way a husband and wife relate. Our homes of origin provide a "school" for marriage.

Siblings, birth order, peers, and society also contribute to our lessons in learning how to love. Basically, love is a learned response, a pattern of actions and reactions observed early in life. Some people are fortunate enough to be raised in emotionally comfortable climates that foster self-worth and emotional security. Each new experience fosters personal growth and eventually a combination of attitudes and sensations develops that gives these people the ability to love and be loved. When two people who fall in love are from similar backgrounds and have developed similar love patterns, their chance for happiness far exceeds the chance for a couple from totally dissimilar backgrounds who have developed different ideas about how to express love.

All is not lost, however, because of improper parental modeling. What is learned can be unlearned and/or replaced with new, more positive behavior.

Love's Mysterious Symptoms

During the romantic phase of falling in love, people usually experience a wide range of feelings and responses, including intense passion and idealization of the partner. This romantic phase, also called infatuation, includes curious emotional and physiological changes—changes that are laboratory tested and 100 percent real. For instance, the sense of being in love makes a woman appear more beautiful. Research explains that "men and women who are in love walk more erectly and appear to have grown taller because the spinal column is stretched." All motor responses are intensely activated, making lovers extremely aware and emotionally receptive.[2]

The production of tears is stepped-up, making eyes appear shinier when in love. This explains why eyes actually appear to sparkle and the world seems brighter and shinier. The heart beats faster, which makes people more susceptible to falling in love. Furthermore, when in love, a person's general health improves, especially for men. Men in unhappy marriages have more heart attacks than those in happy marriages. Those in love also have more energy. Being in love spurs the production of epinephrine (adrenaline) and gives energy and strength to surmount problems.[3]

Another study showed that this increased adrenaline actually makes the heart grow fonder. Participants in this research project were injected with adrenaline to approximate the aroused state of being in love. It was found that these people demonstrated more affection than control subjects who did not have the extra spurt of adrenaline supplied by an injection. In other words, the state of being in love increases the ability to love.[4]

People in love are open to and accepting of what life has to offer. They are ready to enjoy life to its fullest. Such a receptive attitude to the world is called a "YES reaction."

In contrast, those who are not in love present "NO reactions" to others when hurt or angry. Such responses include holding their arms close to their bodies, taking small steps, pursing their lips, and keeping their heads down. They withdraw physically and emotionally from people. In response to their withdrawal, others actually withdraw from them. The result is unhappy persons who don't receive the love and attention they need to make them happy.

A newly divorced person or one who has despaired of ever marrying is often puzzled over why he receives further rejection from everyone he meets. In reality each is probably sending out NO reactions to prospective dates.[5]

Memory improves when one is in love. The person in love possesses an extraordinary ability to remember everything and anything about the loved one. He may forget to pay his rent and she may forget to set her alarm, but neither will forget minutiae about the other. When a person is in love, the mind apparently becomes selective about what it remembers.

Those in love want to be physically close to their loved one. If your partner is constantly edging closer, always wanting to be at your side, chances are she is in love with you or thinks she is.

Love affects brain chemistry. One study concluded that once the emotional state has been defined as "love," there is an increase in the brain chemical phenylethylamine that maintains the emotional high. Interestingly enough, phenylethylamine is the same chemical compound found in chocolate, a popular gift for those in love.[6]

Love also affects eating habits. Many people experience a loss of appetite in the early stages of love. One woman laughingly told me that if she could just stay in love forever she would never have to diet again! Others feel as if they are walking on air or being transported to another world where they are barely conscious of their surroundings.

Lovers may have sweaty hands, butterflies in the stomach, dilated pupils, and so on. Such physiological effects tend to fade in time. Personally, I am glad about that. I'd be exhausted after forty years of going through all that every time Harry walked through the door!

Early in the relationship it is customary to think about the loved one constantly. Lana says dreamily, "I go to sleep thinking about him and he is the first thought that pops into my mind in the morning. Then I begin another day where he is never out of my thoughts." This intense focus on the loved one tends to add even more interest and excitement to the relationship. When separated it is common for a couple in this early romantic phase to anxiously wait for a phone call or reunion with the loved one.

People in this stage talk endlessly about their loved one with anyone who will listen. It is possible that the person may become so totally immersed in the love relationship that responsibilities are ignored or forgotten. Kurt said, "I'm having real difficulty concentrating on my work. It piles up and I can't even force myself to tackle it. I'm getting next to nothing done. The other day I was at a board meeting. Someone asked a question. I didn't even know someone was talking to me until everyone laughed."

Idealization

A person in love tends to idealize the perfection of the loved one. I distinctly remember this phase of my own relationship. Harry was considerate and thoughtful, in contrast to my strict and controlling father. I thought Harry's interest in my every word was wonderful. I insisted that in every way Harry was absolutely perfect for me.

I wanted to see the best in Harry. I concentrated on his positive traits and ignored negative ones. I saw only positive qualities and strengths and imagined these traits growing under my love and encouragement. If I noticed a negative behavior, I tended to excuse it with, "That's not really him" or "That really doesn't matter" or "I can live with that." This is normal for someone in love but it's back to the love-conquers-all theory.

Hollywood and the mass media advance this theory through repeated stories of couples who battle every obstacle and still live "happily ever after." We dream of our own storybook romance and put up with problems and disappointments in our relationship to keep the romantic dream going—sometimes far beyond reality.

There is a tendency to overlook shortcomings. Andre may notice that Tonya doesn't seem to enjoy going places. Tonya says she prefers being alone with Andre. Andre is adventurous and loves to be on the go. He tells himself that Tonya will change in time.

125

Sara notices that Sam spends money carelessly. She excuses such behavior, thinking he will change after they are married, have children, and build their dream home.

Some couples while dating feel secure enough to discuss shortcomings with a partner; others do not. Judy thinks that if she talks with Jeff about a shortcoming, he might get uptight. Her communication with Jeff is already unpredictable. She notices that he is extremely susceptible to a hint of criticism. This could really upset things. So she puts off discussing areas that trouble her. This is the price she is willing to pay for maintaining the relationship. Judy will pay a dear price if she marries Jeff under these circumstances, because they have never learned the communication skills necessary to negotiate differences.

> *It is best to be off with the old love before you go on with the new.*
>
> Great Thoughts,
> Funny Sayings

While the person in love tends to idealize his partner, family members and friends may recognize problems. Karen's parents don't think Jake is the right one for her because he appears controlling and they tell her so; but Karen doesn't want to see or hear it. She wants to believe only the best about Jake.

Jake's best friend may mention to Jake how moody Karen appears and that some of her attitudes are difficult to take. Jake may laugh it off by saying that's what he likes about her.

Marita's best friend warns her constantly about Carlos, who is married. Marita believes that Carlos will leave his wife soon and she refuses to deal with the reality of what dating her while he's married says about his character.

Each one of these people idealizes his or her partner, refusing to see him or her in anything but the best possible light. During the early stages of romance people defend their loved one from the criticism of others and they tend to be blind to objective evaluation. People in these early stages should listen to the candid observations of others precisely because it is so easy to be blinded by romance. Outside evaluation by a party not emotionally involved is essential!

Falling in Love

If you ask people why they got married, most will say, "Because we fell in love." A more accurate statement might be: "We married because we experienced a feeling we interpreted as love." We talk about *falling* in love, but the word *fall* has many meanings. We say: Don't *fall* down; a soldier *falls* in battle; the temperature *falls*; night *falls*; a nation *falls*; someone *falls* ill. What does it mean, then, to *fall* in love?

Generally speaking it means that a couple has connected romantically. This usually means that the feelings of love have hit unexpectedly and the couple are unable to control those feelings. If they have no control over these feelings, it relieves them of any responsibility connected with the romantic state into which they have fallen.

What foolishness! When a couple falls in love, it should not imply that they have fallen into a trap or a pit. We can have control of all our emotions, including love.

The phrase *falling in love* also implies falling into love with the heart only. But falling in love with the heart is only a portion of the love process. Falling in love will involve your head as well as your heart.

How much wiser it is to say that we *grow into love*. Although you may fall into a traumatic condition of infatuation, love takes time to develop. Love is complex. It does not strike unexpectedly, like a star falling from the heavens. True love comes only when two individuals have reoriented their lives, each with the other as a new focal point.

Men usually fall in love much more rapidly than do women. In one study of 250 men and 429 women, researchers measured the "romance quota" of all who were currently in love or recovering from a love affair. One noticeable finding was that more than one quarter of the men said they had fallen seriously in love before the fourth date, while only 15 percent of the women had. In fact, half of the women reported they had not decided if it was genuine love after twenty dates. These women wanted more time.[7]

Men fall in love more rapidly, researchers say, because they are initially attracted by the physical qualities of a woman. One study conducted at a singles bar concluded that men took only seven seconds to decide if they wanted to pursue a relationship with a woman. Men rarely feel an urgency to evaluate a woman over time when her looks are appealing. If she sets his hormones racing, he knows it's love. Thoughts of her homemaking abilities, how she'll look in twelve years after three children, or what kind of a mother she'll make all take a backseat.

A man is more likely to conclude it's love when the woman makes him feel good about himself. This satisfies his most basic emotional need—admiration and appreciation. To find real love, then, men must slow down and love a woman patiently and tenderly over a long period of time. A man who rushes ahead of a woman's instincts may lose in the end.

Women look at love differently than do men. Generally women take longer to decide and aren't as willing to declare undying love until they have assessed a man's inner qualities. They look for characteristics they desire in the father of their children. Women, more than men, have an ability to look into the future and visualize what a marriage will be like.

Women may take longer to fall in love because they are more in touch with their feelings. It is easier for them to distinguish between infatuation, with its rush of emotions, and genuine love, which tends to move more slowly. Women definitely feel and enjoy the tingling and palpitations of infatuation but are more prone to allow their heads to rule their hearts—at least initially.

128

Women are slower than men to label their feelings "love" but are more relentless in their pursuit of the real thing. Once a woman decides she has found the man for her, she is likely to become more intensely emotional and romantic than will a man. Now love becomes euphoric. All life has a special glow. Colors are brighter; she is happier and more beautiful and bubbly than ever before. It is difficult for her to concentrate on anything except her man and dreams of their future together.

Destructive Tactics

Some people are so desperate for love they will resort to devious tactics to try to make a person fall in love with them.

Threats of suicide. Suicide is the most desperate of all attempts to attract someone's attention or get sympathy. Such attempts either end up fatally—in which case the victim will never know if he was really loved—or become proof positive that the person attempting suicide is mentally unbalanced. One woman swallowed a bottle of aspirin only to wake up a day later still alone. Her boyfriend wasn't there and had no intention of coming back. She admitted she never meant to kill herself. No one in his right mind makes a commitment to a suicidal person.

Threats of pregnancy. "I wanted to get married so bad I told my boyfriend I was pregnant," a nurse told me. "He was from an honorable family, and we married immediately. Then I had to make up more lies about an early miscarriage. After one child, it ended in divorce anyway. I know now he never loved me." Even if you could get someone to marry you through such trickery, you would never know if he married you because he really loved you or because of the pregnancy.

Bribes. A thirty-eight-year-old dental hygienist told me that she gave her boyfriend money hoping that he would eventually marry her. "He charged over six thousand dollars on credit cards, eventually left me, and quickly married someone else." Others bribe their loves with trips, expensive cars, clothing, houses, and boats. It may work for a while, but you'll find in the long run you can't buy love.

Jealousy. Some people try to provoke jealousy by pretending there is someone else. They lie and invent other devious plans to capture the attention of a special person. Such plans invariably fail.

Using relatives. Others try to endear themselves to family members and make themselves indispensable. They send cards, presents, and pictures to all the relatives of family events they have attended.

Some people want to get married so badly they will do anything or say anything to snare a spouse. But few who are worth having will listen to groveling, sniveling, lying, bribery, or threats. Rather than attracting someone by such tactics, one gives evidence of low self-esteem and insecurity. Resorting to destructive tactics rarely wins committed love.

Love Styles

When two people fall in love, they express their love for each other through a certain pattern of actions and behaviors. These behaviors have been studied by Lobsenz and Lasswell and fall into six basic patterns or "love styles."[8]

Best Friends

A relationship that grows over a long period of time between a couple who spend a great deal of time together in a totally nonromantic way, at least to begin with, is called Best Friends. The relationship is built on companionship, sharing of mutual concerns, and eventually self-disclosure and intimacy. In the beginning neither thinks of the relationship as romantic. The relationship tends to be more tender, caring, and thoughtful than a passionate love affair. An argument between Best Friends is discussed rationally and negotiated in a friendly manner. The two avoid outright conflict. Intense feelings of anger or love are out of range for Best Friends. Generally speaking those who love within the Best Friends style are products of emotionally secure parents where companionship, warmth, and support knit the family together. The commitment to each other is strong in this style.

The Game Player

The Game Player thinks of love as a contest where competition, skill, and winning dominate. Strategies and tactical moves keep the relationship interesting. The object of the game is friendly play, encouraging intimacy without getting too close. Commitment is virtually impossible. Frequently the Game Player will be promiscuous prior to marriage and may continue to be so after marriage. Challenge and risk are important to continue the game situation. Fighting and flirting are common occurrences. The Game Player places few demands on a partner and gives little. This love style is self-centered and exploitative.

Logical Love

When a person concentrates on the realistic, practical value that can be found in a relationship, this is logical love. This person comes with a carefully thought-out list of desired qualities and requirements for a partner. He knows what he wants in appearance, education, family, religious background, personality, and character. He also knows what he has to offer and attempts to make a fair exchange. Computer dating services appeal to this type. Logical Lovers find it easy to postpone or avoid love until they have analytically assessed all the pros and cons. They plan their love life, using the same techniques they have used to map out educational, recreational, and business pursuits. When the partner views this logical perspective as an attribute and not a liability, the two will get along well, all other factors being equal.

Possessive Love

Possessive Love is a limiting and unfulfilling love style. The Possessive Lover has an obsessive need to prove to himself over and over that he is the object of his partner's affections. Mood swings from elation to despair, from devotion to jealousy are common. The Possessive Lover lavishes attention on his loved one and desires constant togetherness. This can be flattering early in a relationship. Intense jealousy is viewed as evidence of love by some, particularly in the early stages of romance. Later on, though, such possessiveness or jealousy may get on the partner's nerves. An obsessive need for togetherness and "proof" of love reveals emotional insecurity and low self-worth.

Romantic Love

Those who view their relationship through rose-colored glasses are in Romantic Love. They are the love-conquers-all lovers. They believe their love can surmount any problem and they expect a constant series of emotional highs. Romantic Lovers believe in love at first sight. They spot each other across a crowded room. Physical attraction holds a high priority in Romantic Love as do gifts, flowers, and other romantic gestures.

Romantic Love is too intense to last. If a couple marries on the basis of romantic love alone, they will be unprepared to deal with the natural tapering off of romantic feelings that occurs shortly after marriage. The disillusionment following the loss of such intensity must be replaced by something—acceptance of the loss, working toward rekindling romantic excitement, or substituting romantic fantasies.

Unselfish Love

The sixth and final love style is Unselfish Love, which is characterized by giving, forgiving, and caring. It is a nurturing love that can deny self to give to the other. Such a love survives even when emotional pain is created by the one loved. This love puts the needs of the other before its own. It delights more in giving than in receiving.

Rather than having only one love style, most people are a combination of two or more styles. There is little research to indicate that those with similar love styles enjoy a more stable relationship than those with differing styles. But this isn't what's important. The key factor is whether we understand our combination of styles and those of the people we date and the one we eventually marry. A couple who have the same style can more easily understand each other's behavior. Those with a different combination of styles can do likewise if they can learn to fulfill each other's needs even though it may not be as easy and natural. A couple with the same love style can become bored with one another, while differing styles can produce irritation, emotional pain, and unfulfilled needs.

Women usually fit into the Logical, Possessive, and Best Friend styles, while men are often comfortable in the Game Playing and Romantic styles. The same percentage of men and women use the Unselfish style. According to researchers, a combination of Best Friends and Unselfish styles is as close to ideal as a couple can come. Even then patience, acceptance, sensitivity, and understanding must be exhibited to meet each other's differing needs.

The more different the styles—for example, a Possessive Lover and a Game Player or a Romantic Lover and a Game Player—the more frustration and pain the couple will experience. Should they marry, they will likely get divorced because at the very core level neither is able to meet the other's basic emotional needs.

No one's personal style is cast in cement. We can learn to adapt and provide the type of love our partner needs. But it takes maturity and self-worth to do this kind of adapting and the best time to do it is before marriage, not afterward. Some love styles are healthier than others to begin with. Those with a Possessive or Game Player style must seek a greater understanding of what love means if they want to have a fulfilling love relationship.

How can we develop a healthier love style? By practicing the presence of Jesus Christ in our lives. Even though we may have experienced emotional abuse or insecurity in our childhood and have lifelong scars, Jesus can meet our needs and heal our wounds. It is possible to achieve a positive, healthy emotional balance as adults as we allow the Savior to work in our lives and change us.

Answers to True Love Test, pp. 116–17: 1–F, 2–F, 3–F, 4–F, 5–T, 6–T, 7–T, 8–T, 9–F, 10–F, 11–F, 12–F, 13–T, 14–F, 15–F, 16–F, 17–F, 18–F, 19–F, 20–F

8

Love or Infatuation

Discerning the Difference

S tudies show that most people tend to rate past relationships as infatuation and present relationships as real love. Undoubtedly many past romances would have been described as love if the study had been conducted while the romances were in progress. Another survey found that in her lifetime the average person experiences infatuation six or seven times and real love only once or twice.

The dictionary defines infatuation as "a foolish, extravagant, all-absorbing passion; irrational love or desire; blind love." It comes from a Latin word meaning "silly or foolish," which graphically describes some people's behavior. However foolish, the experience can be wildly exciting. Infatuation feels the same as love and the intensity of feelings is just as strong in both. That's the trouble: Infatuation appears real. This is true at thirty-seven or at fifty-seven.

Differentiating between love and infatuation is always complicated because both conditions share three similar symptoms: passion, a desire to be close, and strange emotions.

Passion: Passion may be present without genuine love. It is entirely possible, particularly for the male, to feel passionate or to have strong sexual feelings for a woman he has never met. Body fondling and passionate kissing increase the urgency of erotic feelings until the relationship is mainly sexual. Passion does not necessarily indicate genuine love. Sexual attraction can be as urgent in infatuation as it is in genuine love. Sometimes it is the major part of infatuation. Love, however, is always based on more than sex, including shared interests, values, goals, and beliefs.

Infatuation is a stage that is too intense to last. Neither a man nor a woman can maintain such fierce passion for long, although they vow they will. If all a couple has going for them is passion, the relationship will likely end in three to six months. Couples who marry based on this initial rush find that when the passion dies there is nothing left to hold them together.

Desire to be close: The desire to be near one another constantly can be just as overwhelming in infatuation as in genuine love. You may wish to be together all the time, dreading the time when you must part. You may feel empty and lonely when your loved one is not with you, but this does not necessarily mean that it is real love.

Strange emotions: Researchers agree on certain distinct physical symptoms at the onset of infatuation as documented in the last chapter. Strange emotions can occur just as frequently with infatuation as with real love, although "funny feelings" and strange emotions are probably more indicative of infatuation. Genuine love encompasses more than a mixture of giggly or sick feelings and will continue long after such strange feelings subside.

Certain life experiences make people more vulnerable to infatuation. Those who are lonely or bored or are struggling to overcome the hurt of a broken romance or the rejection of divorce often interpret infatuation as real love. Those who are insecure and suffer from low self-esteem must also beware. Although secure and levelheaded people can be deceived by infatuation, they are more likely to recognize the condition for what it is.

Please note that infatuation is not bad. It can be a pleasant and enjoyable experience as long as you recognize it for what it is—a brief interlude of romantic fantasy that cannot last. Given enough time, it will pass or it will develop into a real relationship that is more than a rush of emotions.

Mature love differs from infatuation in that it gives a person time and space to recognize the good qualities and shortcomings of the loved one. To move in with someone or to marry on the basis of these early feelings, especially if a couple is already sexually intimate, is sheer foolishness and invites predictable, negative consequences.

Testing for Love

In the 1820s greenhorn gold rush prospectors occasionally mistook pyrite for gold. Pyrite, or fool's gold as it is called, can be detected by popping it into a pan and putting it on a hot stove. While it sizzles and smokes it sends out a strong stench. But heat will not damage real gold nor does it smell foul. Unfortunately you cannot put your love relationship in a pan on a hot stove to see if it produces a stench but you can test it against the following twelve factors. They are not listed in order of importance. Consider each factor as objectively as you can.

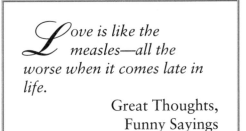

Love is like the measles—all the worse when it comes late in life.

Great Thoughts,
Funny Sayings

1. *Love develops slowly; infatuation rapidly.* Falling in love is often described as happening suddenly and intensely.

137

One study indicated that more than 50 percent of adults reported falling in love at first sight at least once in their life.

Jermaine reported, "I knew it when I saw her. She looked just as I always pictured she would. On that first date we talked half the night and I felt as if I'd known her all my life. There was a feeling of incredible closeness that I've never experienced with anyone else. I'm convinced that dreams really do come true!"

Jermaine may be convinced early in the relationship that dreams come true but his evaluation won't be valid until after a year of dating. Why? Because love grows and growth requires time. It's infatuation that hits swiftly and suddenly. It is impossible to know the real person after only a few meetings. Early in a relationship people wear masks while putting on their best behavior. Any unpleasant traits are closely guarded, hidden, and controlled. For this reason it takes months and even years of seeing a person under varied circumstances before it can be said you know someone really well. Many people successfully hide negative personality traits until after marriage. This is why some people complain they married a stranger.

Don't jump to conclusions. Allow your relationship to grow slowly. Begin as friends and don't hurry the love stage. Leisurely beginnings can be pleasurable and much safer. Eventually such friendships can lead to ecstasy that resembles infatuation in intensity but is rooted in reality.

2. *Love relies on compatibility; infatuation relies more on chemistry and physical appearance.* Steve met someone new, interesting, and good-looking. The initial small talk went well. He got a good feeling—there was definitely a chemistry between them. "Either it works or it doesn't," Steve says with a shrug. "You either feel it or you don't. Your heart races or it doesn't. I felt it."

If only discovering genuine love were as easy as Steve thinks it is! Where did Steve come up with the idea that chemistry and love are the same thing? Probably from romantic love scenes portrayed in the media—the script reads, "Her heart raced with excitement, she melted into his arms, and their bodies merged."

It's likely that more people pretend this happens than actually experience it. More likely they are conditioned for it and it happens because they desire it intensely. Many who marry because of chemistry wake up later to deal with disastrous relationships. Relying on chemistry alone to guide you toward love is dangerous.

This is true because chemistry is based mostly on physical or sexual attraction. I believe there needs to be that spark and pull between the two of you that make your eyes light up and make you feel more alive than you have ever felt before, but to base a relationship on this alone is ludicrous.

Is there such a thing as love-at-first-sight? I can accept "like-at-first-sight" or even "like-very-much-at-first-sight," but _love?_ No. You may feel strongly about and be passionately attracted to a person you have just met but that is chemistry. You like what you see—body build, actions, responses. You may like everything about the person, but there is still a long way to go before you and this person have developed real love.

Although genuine love includes chemistry and physical attraction, it springs from many other factors as well, including character, personality, emotions, ideas, and attitudes. When you're in love you are interested in the way the object of your love thinks and responds to situations. You will focus on the values you hold in common. How does the other person respond to personal success or failure? to the pitfalls and challenges of life? Is he or she kind, appreciative, and courteous? Do your attitudes on religion, family, sex, finances, and friends match? What interests do you share in common? Can you enjoy an evening with family or friends at home or must you always go out somewhere? Are your backgrounds similar? The more you have in common in these areas, the better your chances are for developing genuine love. Compatible personalities, along with common interests and values, go a long way toward developing a lasting love relationship.

3. *Love centers on one person only; infatuation may involve several persons.* An infatuated person may be "in love" with two or more persons at the same time. These individuals may differ markedly in personality and temperament. For instance, Jan says she is in love with two men and finds it impossible to choose between them. One is sensible, stable, and responsible; the other is an irresponsible, fun-loving spendthrift. Most likely Jan is in love with neither one. Something in her draws her to the fun-loving spender while another part tells her that the qualities of stability and responsibility are more important. Genuine love focuses on one person in whose character and personality are found the qualities you believe are most essential.

4. *Love produces security; infatuation produces insecurity.* When in love, a person has a sense of security and trust after considering all the factors in the relationship. An infatuated person, on the other hand, struggles with feelings of insecurity and may attempt to control the loved one through jealousy. This does not mean that when you really love someone you will never feel jealous. In a love relationship that has developed over time, however, jealousy is less frequent and less severe. Love trusts.

As I said earlier, some may feel flattered by jealousy at first. They think it indicates true love and assume that the more jealous a lover is, the more in love he is. Jealousy, however, does not signify healthy emotions, but rather insecurity and a poor self-image. Whatever the root cause, a jealous person wants to fence the other person in, keeping her to himself. Jealousy produces selfishness and possessiveness. Real love doesn't act this way.

5. *Love recognizes realities; infatuation ignores them.* Genuine love looks at problems squarely without trying to minimize their seriousness. Infatuation ignores differences

140

in social, racial, educational, or religious backgrounds. Sometimes infatuation grips a person who is already married or is in a situation that precludes open dating. Infatuation causes a couple to disregard or gloss over differences. If you love each other, things can be worked out, they think.

A couple in love face problems frankly and they attempt to solve them. If problems threaten their relationship, they discuss them openly and decide on intelligent solutions. A couple in love anticipate problems most likely to occur and negotiate solutions in advance.

6. _Love motivates positive behavior; infatuation has a destructive effect._ Love will have a constructive effect on your personality and bring out the very best in you. It will give you new energy, ambition, and interest in life. Love promotes creativity and interest in personal growth, improvement, and worthy causes. It engenders feelings of self-worth, trust, and security. Love will spur you on toward success. You will work harder, plan more effectively, and save more diligently. When you are in love, life takes on additional purpose and meaning. You may daydream about the future but you stay within the bounds of reality by centering your thoughts on plans within reach. Your love encourages you to function at your highest level.

By contrast, infatuation has a destructive and disorganizing effect on the personality. You will find yourself less effective, less efficient, less able to reach your true potential. Family members or close friends may notice this effect immediately. They may say, "What's come over you? You won't go anywhere or do anything. What's the matter? Are you sick or something?" Then someone else will comment, "No, she's not sick. She's in love." That observation is incorrect—you are infatuated, not in love.

Infatuation thrives on unrealistic dreams in which the two of you lead a beautiful, blissful life in perfect agreement. These dreams cause you to forget the realities of life, work, responsibilities, and money.

*T*he 1950s saw the advent of the "Puppy Love Anklet." If you wore the anklet on the right ankle, that meant you were available. If you wore the anklet on the left ankle, you were going steady.

Curious Facts

7. *Love recognizes faults; infatuation ignores them.* If you are in love, you will naturally idealize your love but this will tend to grow out of an understanding and appreciation for the other person that has been checked against reality. Love leads you to recognize the fine qualities in the other person and helps you build a relationship based on them. Even though you recognize those good qualities and idealize them to some degree, the person is not seen as without fault. You admit your loved one falls short of perfection but you see so much to respect and admire that you accept the person on the basis of the good qualities.

If you are infatuated, you idealize with complete disregard for reality. Infatuation keeps you from seeing anything wrong with the one you love and you are unable to admit that he has faults. You defend him against all critics. You admire one or two qualities so much that you fool yourself into believing that these can outweigh all faults or problems.

Rhonda began to wake up when Eric failed to pick her up for a job interview as promised. She missed the appointment and had no chance for the job. A year later he was still forgetting things, making up excuses, and failing to show up as promised. Rhonda finally broke off the relationship, but why did she wait so long?

Some people want love so badly they live in denial, shielding themselves from fears they think they can't handle. Love recognizes the good but is not blind to problem areas in the loved one's personality.

8. *Love controls physical contact; infatuation exploits it.* Since real love and respect are almost synonymous, a couple who genuinely love each other will tend to hold in check

their expression of physical affection. Each respects the other so much that they voluntarily put on hold their desire for sexual intercourse. The desire is present but it is under control. Expressions of physical affection comprise a small part of the total relationship for a couple in love, in contrast to an infatuated couple. The relationship of an infatuated couple depends largely on physical attraction and physical and emotional excitement. People may enjoy feelings they've never felt before or have not felt in a long time and conclude they are in love.

When men or women experience a strong sexual attraction to a partner and assume they are in love, they may marry on the basis of sexual excitement alone. They ignore the fact that their values, goals, and belief systems are at odds. They may have few common interests and incompatible personalities and character traits. As their relationship continues they will probably discover they differ on many aspects of life, from what to do on a day off to how to spend money. Not only is their interest in each other on the wane, but they doubt that they even like each other. In the midst of such chaos they find their sexual interest also declining. When they finally wake up to what everyone else could see all along, they part. They weren't in love; they were "in lust."

For the couple in love, physical contact usually has a deeper meaning than sheer pleasure. It expresses how they feel toward each other. Unfortunately, for many couples body fondling along with sexual intercourse are often the basis for the relationship. The search for pleasure dominates.

9. *Love is selfless; infatuation is selfish.* Being in love involves more than just the emotions. Genuine love is acted out in everyday life. You expect to be treated with love and consideration and you also express love and consideration to your partner, even when you don't feel like it. Any of us can be loving when our needs are met and our partner behaves in a loving manner. But the test of love is whether you can be loving even when your partner has treated you

143

unfairly, neglected your needs, forgotten your birthday, or been inconsiderate.

One of my favorite *Peanuts* cartoons shows Charlie Brown dressed in pajamas carrying a glass of water to Snoopy, who is lazily perched on top of his doghouse. The caption reads: "Love is getting someone a glass of water in the middle of the night." Chuck has the right idea. It isn't easy to get up in the middle of the night and put someone else's needs before your own.

Infatuation is self-centered. You think more in terms of what the relationship can do for you than what you can do for the other person. You enjoy the feeling of pride you have when your partner is with you and others realize she belongs to you.

10. *Love brings the approval of family and friends; infatuation brings disapproval.* The divorce rate in Japan is one fourth the divorce rate in the United States. The fact that most Japanese choose partners who are approved by their families, while American couples choose regardless of family approval, may explain the discrepancy. Apparently Japanese families have a clearer vision of who is suitable than the adult child has on her own. When your family and close friends see that you are well suited to your partner, they will usually approve. They will see how well your personalities blend, the many interests you share, and how you complement and motivate each other.

> *If you kiss a toad, you don't get a prince— you get slime in your mouth and bad memories.*
>
> Laura Schlessinger

If your parents or friends do not approve, beware! If they are convinced that the one you have chosen is wrong for you, they are probably right. Family and friends are extremely interested in your future welfare and don't want you to get hurt. Since they are not as emotionally involved as you, they may be able to see certain aspects you can't see.

144

Statistics show that marriages that lack the blessing of parents have a high failure rate. One researcher compared complaints registered by happily married persons with those of divorced persons. Divorced individuals were almost four times as likely to complain that their spouse had little in common with mutual friends. It was also found that happily married couples were far less likely to have problems with each other's parents. If parents and friends object, take care. If they approve, take heart. There's a good chance you have found genuine love.

11. *Love ends slowly; infatuation ends rapidly.* You cannot test this factor, of course, until the relationship ends. But in retrospect a person can ask two questions: How long did the romance last? And how long did it take for me to get over it? Just as genuine love takes time to develop, so it also takes time for such feelings to vanish. It can happen in no other manner. If the two of you have grown and shared many experiences together, you may not get over a breakup for a long period of time.

Infatuations end much the same way they begin—fast—with one exception. Infatuation will not end rapidly if you have become involved sexually. Sex complicates the emotional responses. A couple may stay together not because of genuine love but because of mutually satisfying sexual relations. Therefore the length of time it takes to recover from a breakup does not indicate anything significant if the couple is sexually involved.

12. *Love survives the test of time; infatuation can't wait.* Infatuation wants to rush the relationship. Pulsating emotions overrule good sense and people rush into commitments that may be regretted in all the years to come.

Don't make quick commitments that you will regret later. True love can survive the test of time.

Even though your sexual urges are exploding and throbbing at an all-time high, hold off sexual involvement. Sex now will confuse the emotions and complicate the process of separating infatuation from the real thing. This calls for self-denial, patience, and discipline—traits that go a long way in building a relationship that lasts.

Given time, infatuation may grow into genuine love. So there is no reason to end the relationship the minute you diagnose infatuation. Severing ties immediately, without allowing the initial intense feelings to run their course, may preclude knowing if infatuation would lead to true love.

Adopt a wait-and-see attitude. If the relationship lasts a year—great. During the second year carefully evaluate the factors of your partner's personality as well as your own. Relationships involving a previously married person and stepchildren require more time and evaluation than others.

A six- to nine-month engagement period is needed to give a couple time to prepare for a wedding, but more important, to prepare for a lifetime relationship. In-depth guidance with a qualified counselor should be pursued. These sessions, which extend over several weeks, should include a series of discussions, outside reading, personality testing, and written homework.

Such an approach to marriage may sound clinical and unromantic, but where such programs have been implemented, a divorce rate of only 3 to 5 percent is reported. Compare this to the national average of 50 percent!

To win the love and respect of their partner, most people show only their better sides and attempt to hide their faults and shortcomings. They believe that if the other person knew about their faults or idiosyncrasies they would not be good enough or lovable enough. So they act a part, act like these faults are not a part of themselves—for a time—allowing their loved one to see them only at their best. My term for this behavior is *masking*.

Since it is difficult to play a role or wear a mask for long periods of time, it eventually becomes tiresome and the mask will slip. This is when you can begin to see some of the hidden traits in your partner. So it is important to stay in a relationship long enough for the masks to slip. It may be possible for a person to mask a fault for a year, but for longer than that would be difficult. It is for this reason that I strongly urge couples to go together for two years. During the first year you are measuring compatibility and waiting to see the masks slip. After the masks slip, you begin to see the real person. Then decide if the good qualities outweigh the negative qualities now appearing. To marry someone before the masks have slipped is like marrying a stranger. You simply do not know what you are getting or what unpleasant surprises lie ahead.

If you analyze your situation carefully but still can't decide whether or not you have found true love; if the more you try, the more confused you get, allow yourself more time. Time will give you experience and perspective as it offers more contact with your friend. It will provide more opportunities for you to find out what you need to know to make the final decision. When all is said and done, you have found lifetime love when your mutual relationship fosters individual growth for both of you and increases the depth of your love for each other.

More than a million divorces occur annually in the United States. The average duration of these marriages is seven years. Half of them disintegrate within three years after the wedding. Each of these couples stood at the altar, eyes bright with joy, promising love and faithfulness forever, never anticipating that they were making the greatest mistake of their lives. What happened to their starry-eyed talks, the tender promises, lingering looks, close embraces, passionate kisses, and whispers of love?

Most failed to understand that you don't "fall" in love. You decide to love—to think about, spend time with, and have strong feelings for someone. "Falling" is the easy and fun part of love. The hard part, the commitment to love unconditionally an imperfect person, follows. Genuine love says, "I will love you unconditionally even when you fail to meet my needs, reject or ignore me, behave stupidly, make choices I wouldn't have made, hurt me, disagree with me, and treat me unfairly. And I will love you like this forever." This is what genuine love is and it involves much more than sexual excitement or infatuation. Infatuation is little more than a cheap substitute for the real thing. Attempting to build a relationship on infatuation is risky, to say the least.

This doesn't mean you should view all romantic involvements with fear or suspicion. An exciting infatuation can be fun and a glorious booster to self-worth while making you feel younger and more alive than you've felt in years. When you find one, enjoy it rather than fighting it. Just don't allow your pulsating emotions to overrule good sense! Call it by its right name—infatuation—not love.

Biblical Love

We've been looking at the way society views love, but what does Scripture say about love? In the New Testament five Greek words are used to define love.[1]

Epithymia is never translated "love" yet it is an important part of love. It means a strong desire of any kind or to long for or even covet. When translated in a negative way, it is the equivalent of lust. Within marriage, *epithymia* means the strong physical desire a couple has that results in sexual intercourse.

Eros is sensual love. It means devoted to or arousing sexual desire. To feel eros is to be strongly affected by sexual desire. It can be controlled and positive, or uncontrolled and sinful. It is the desire to unite with and possess the loved one. The English word *erotic* is derived from the word *eros*. Whereas erotic love is important within marriage, outside of marriage erotic love engenders neither the commitment nor the staying power needed to hold a relationship together. It is based solely on intense physical feelings. Feelings of *eros* can be selfish and self-serving.

A third type of love, _storge,_ describes natural affection and a feeling of belonging to each other. Loyalty and commitment are fulfilled through _storge_ love.

Phileo is friendship love, a type of love that should have high priority in marriage and long before. It means companionship, communication, cooperation, and pure enjoyment in being with someone called "friend." Thoughts, attitudes, experiences, feelings, and dreams are shared through _phileo_ love. It cherishes and enjoys the presence of the other.

Agape love, the highest type of love expressed in the Bible, values and serves the loved one. It loves the unlovable. It keeps erotic love alive and possesses the power to rekindle what has died. It is an act of the will, not based on feelings. _Agape_ love is a deep reservoir that provides stability even during times of stress and conflict. It is perhaps best described by God's love for us as exemplified in John 3:16. _Agape_ love originates from God, not from within us. _Agape_ love costs. God models this love for us throughout Scripture. It is an art that may take a lifetime to learn.

Genuine love has a bit of all five types of love in it but is dominated by _agape_ love. To experience this kind of love, you have to be willing to risk being rejected or feeling unloved. It means wanting the best for your loved one even if the best opposes your personal wishes. Love means encouraging and supporting each other's dreams even if it costs you something. It means wanting your partner to achieve and become all he can be even if it becomes threatening to you. Love also means giving security when it is needed as well as space when privacy is desired.

This kind of love is God's creative gift to us and can be enjoyed to its fullest only within the safety and security of marriage. We are only able to love because He first loved us. It is through His love that we are freed from the hurt of past relationships and are willing to risk loving again. Through Him we no longer need to be dominated by rejection and failure.

Even genuine love changes over the years. The intense love you feel for someone now can grow stale or intensify. That's the way love is. It is fragile and needs constant nourishment to flourish. But also remember that in genuine love there's a good measure of *agape* love, which creates a God-like ability to love even when we are not loved in return. It endures, praise God!

Booth Tarkington once said:

> It is love in old age, no longer blind, that is true love. For love's highest intensity doesn't necessarily mean its highest quality. Glamour and jealousy are gone; and the ardent caress, no longer needed, is valueless compared to the reassuring touch of a trembling hand. Passers-by commonly see little beauty in the embrace of young lovers on a park bench, but the understanding smile of an old wife to her husband is one of the loveliest things in the world.

A Fantastic Forever Friend

Society programs us through the mass media and other forums to believe that love will solve all personal problems. Such a concept leads people down a dangerous path because they expect romance to offer what only Jesus can supply.

Rather than securing all your hopes and dreams to a human being, why not secure yourself first and foremost to someone who will never change? Jesus is always the same, yesterday, today, and forever. Any promise He makes, He will keep. You can count on it. His love is completely unconditional. He will always love you regardless of your appearance, failures, or mistakes. When others fail you, He will be there to love and care about you. He is the only one who loves perfectly.

Jesus is the only one who can supply all your needs, fulfill all your desires, and meet all your expectations. Anchor yourself to Him first and then you will be less likely to be disappointed in love and more likely to find a satisfying love for your sojourn on this earth.

Part 5

Close Encounters
of a Dangerous Kind

9

Touchy Situations

Secular research claims that 95 percent of formerly married persons are sexually active. A recent survey of divorced Christians showed only 9 percent of the men and 27 percent of the women had been celibate since the end of their marriages. The remainder were sexually active. One fourth of the men and one half of the women said celibacy was unrealistic and impossible to practice. What a sad indictment!

Since physical intimacy is easier to attain than emotional intimacy, many people begin their relationships with sexual intimacy, hoping they will later learn to be friends. But sex outside of marriage derails a relationship. When physical desire escalates, it dominates all other aspects of relationship building. Those who want to get close fast use the easy road—sex. But rather than drawing the couple together, sex steals the show and produces a counterfeit closeness.

Reggie and Yvonne were powerfully attracted to each other at first sight and drifted to Yvonne's place after their first date. Each had enjoyed a variety of come-and-go lovers. Why make exceptions now? Their relationship became torrid and exciting, but soon the great love affair of the century became a series of misunderstandings and arguments.

Like Reggie and Yvonne, many people seem to know how to be lovers but they don't know how to be friends. The more physically involved a couple become, the less opportunity there is to develop a friendship or to talk about significant topics that will mold their future.

Many people play at love as if it were a game. Their concept of love is perverted and confused by sex play and sensual gratification. To see how far they can get in a relationship, to see how much personal and sexual fun they can enjoy without getting hurt or trapped by commitment becomes a challenge. Others who play with sex don't know any better. They are insecure and use sexual conquests to boost sagging self-esteem, forget personal problems, or work through hurt from the past. Both sexes play the game but they do so differently.

Sexual Game Playing: Lines Masked and Unmasked

Bill Bradington, a forty-two-year-old salesman, arrives at a party quietly. Bill is good looking but not drop-dead attractive. He's dressed well but not over dressed. Making his way to the food table, he smiles and greets those he already knows. If you watch him carefully, you'll note that his eyes are busy, checking the crowd for a female who is attractive but looks bored or lonely. He spots one and strikes up a conversation. All those sales seminars he's attended come into play now. He's a great talker—charming, funny, and smart.

Bill listens attentively while the woman talks. He compliments her on things she thought no one noticed: a pretty scarf, her hair. He sets off no alarms because he is not aggressive. Women tend to think of him more as a friend than a lover—at least at first.

But make no mistake. Bill is very much aware of what he is doing. And he's using it all—flattery, charm, and attention—to get what he wants. One of Bill's outstanding qualities is that he is patient. His objective is to get a woman to bed when and if she is willing and the circumstances are right.

It's the hunt, chase, and conquest that he really enjoys. Every time he sees her he ingratiates himself a little more— a little more talk, a little more flattery, a little more charm. Six months pass before he makes his move and delivers his favorite line. He engineers a meeting, "accidentally" running into her outside her office. He invites her out for something simple, soup and sandwich, nothing threatening.

Now he's ready to move in for the kill. "Can I tell you something?" he begins slowly with a mysterious smile. "I find you very attractive." It's not very creative, but he's primed her well to this point. And it works. "It's like striking pay dirt," Bill says.

The role of "lines" and other devious tactics used to entice the opposite sex into sex play is stronger than most people realize. Sexual game playing and lines are things said or done to pressure or manipulate the other into having sex. Never underestimate the power of a good line delivered in the heat of passion. Many highly principled people have found themselves victims of a well-timed, well-chosen line. Each person should know how much stock to put in what is said or done at the time and at what point to limit sex play.

Lines Men Use

True love. One study revealed the most prevalent line is: "If you love me, you'll let me." Men have been using this line since the beginning of time. But the real question is, if he does get what he wants, what proof will you have when it is all over that he really loves you? It is more likely that he used you to satisfy his own urgent needs. The one who uses this line is usually a slow but steady operator who tends to hang in there until he gets what he wants. A good response to this line is: "If you really love me, you won't ask."

155

Flattery. "You have such a gorgeous body I can hardly control myself!" Or "You are so beautiful I can hardly take my eyes off you." Or "You have the most beautiful eyes in the world." Under questioning, males who use this line reveal they use it because they can think of little else to say. They simply use flattery to get what they want. An attractive woman enjoys hearing it, and even the most unattractive female feels complimented, so it can work with all types of women. And here's an interesting sidelight: One study showed that sexually aroused males rated pictures of women as much more attractive than did males who were not sexually aroused when viewing the same pictures. In other words, the greater the sexual need, the better any female will look to a man regardless of her appearance.

A good response to this line might be: "Thank you. I'm glad you appreciate my looks but I'm holding out for a man who appreciates something beyond looks."

Sympathy. "My wife divorced me. I deserve it. I'm a mess. Nobody understands me." This guy sings the blues and cries on your shoulder.

The effectiveness of this approach lies in its appeal to the mothering instincts of a woman. This fellow could amount to something with your help. You know about his past but that could change if he just had a chance. You see tremendous potential and vow to give him the opportunity he needs. Whatever the version, beware of this line. This guy has mastered the technique of playing on a woman's sympathies. Just as soon as you begin smothering him with sympathy, he'll begin preparing you for the pushover! One response for this line is: "I understand more than you think I do. What you need is a mother and a good therapist!"

The opposite version of the sympathy approach reads like this: "You poor thing. Life hasn't treated you very well so far. You have a lot of hurt in your past and I'll help you put it all in the past. I'm here now to show you real love, right now, in bed." Any time sympathy is the primary motive, beware. This line poses a special danger for a woman from an unhappy childhood or for one just out of a divorce or unhappy relationship. A woman is extremely vulnerable and an easy target when she is feeling sorry for herself. She needs a man to understand her, of course, but make sure he understands more about life than how to manipulate a woman toward sex.

Situational ethics. "Everybody's doing it. We're not kids anymore. What's the matter with you?" is a line used by the situational ethics crowd. This line implies there is something the matter with a female who won't live the way the rest of the world lives. She is accused of possessing Victorian ideals. "Times have changed," they chant. "Live today and don't look back." Such pressure is put on her that she begins to wonder if she really is the only one who is still holding out in today's world. In the age of AIDS, however, a good response might be: "What's wrong with it? What's RIGHT with it? I want to live not die!"

Big shot. The line goes something like "Women are standing in line for blocks to date me. You better get with it or you might lose me. You don't know how lucky you are to get this opportunity." This probably isn't verbalized in just this manner, but you get the idea through his words and actions. This guy is likely personable, good-looking, athletic, and popular. He has the ability to make a woman feel super special. You will be espe-

> *John McPherson, an Englishman, set a new world's record in 1988 by kissing 4,444 women in eight hours. That's one kiss every 6.48 seconds.* The Guinness Book of World Records *doesn't mention any record for kissing the same person. If it did, the record might go to Sadie Nine and Paul Trevillion. They kissed each other 20,009 times in two hours. To train for such strenuous activity, Sadie and Paul bicycle and they rub their lips with seawater and sunflower oil.*
>
> Curious Facts

cially vulnerable to this type if you are inexperienced in game-playing tactics or if you have a low self-image. A good response is: "I'll pass on this extraordinary opportunity. Reach out and touch someone else!"

Logical. "Honey, we plan on getting married anyway. Our love is greater than any slip of paper. This will prove our love for each other in a special way." This line comes on so gradually that it is sometimes difficult to recognize. It occurs most often in a long-term relationship with a nice man who you *know* is right for you.

A good response to this line would be: "In case we ever changed our minds about each other, I wouldn't want you to feel obligated to me nor do I want to have anything to regret." Then be prepared for protests! One study revealed that more than 33 percent of the sexually active women thought when they first had sex with a man they would marry him—but few did. However, only 7 percent of the males polled thought they would marry the woman. One of two things was taking place—either she was fooling herself or he wasn't telling the truth. Take your pick.

Abnormal. "What's the matter with you? Are you frigid or something? You don't want word to get around that you can't make it, do you?" For a woman who is looking forward to a sexually fulfilling relationship with her husband someday, this plants seeds of doubt about her ability to function. She wonders whether she might be undersexed or undesirable. Warning: Men who use this approach generally think of women as things to be used by males. Chances are the "pro" with this line would and could produce real sexual problems for a woman. A good response might be: "There's nothing the matter with me that forgetting you couldn't cure. You're history, friend."

Intellectual. This fellow promotes heavy think sessions regarding sex. He doesn't do anything at first—just gets you in the habit of talking about sex. He's an excellent conversationalist who can wow you with phrases and ideas. His object is to lead you on in the natural sequence of events. Promoting sexually enlightening discussions can be very stimulating to both of you. Some who use this approach are completely innocent and others are old smoothies. When things get too hot, better call a halt. A good response: "This conversation is getting too hot to handle. Either cool things down or take a hike, a permanent hike."

The threat. "If you don't, I'll date someone else." This line attempts to intimidate you by implying that unless you give in to his desires, you will have to sit at home alone for the rest of your life. He probably won't have any trouble finding a willing partner. But you know now exactly what he wants, and any woman will do. Tell this one: "I'll pass your name around to my friends along with your threat and then I'll look for someone who will appreciate me for something beyond my body."

Promises, promises. "I won't get you pregnant. You won't catch a disease from me! I told you I will never leave you. We will get married someday." Under the pressure of sexual tension, some guys make promises they can't keep. They may mean every word at the moment, but it is surprising how quickly they forget a promise once urgent sexual pressure has been relieved. Women fall for promises because they so desperately want to believe what has been promised. Use a logical response to a promise line: "Are you prepared to be a father should I get pregnant?" or "Let's make absolutely sure that you don't have an STD or AIDS by getting tested at the nearest clinic and then waiting six months."

Guilt. "I'm so tensed up I can't stand it! You've let me go this far. You can't stop now! You're driving me wild! I just gotta have it!" No, he doesn't just gotta have it. If he doesn't get a sexual release right then, nothing detrimental will happen to him. He will not suffer brain damage, develop a hernia, or go bald. The worst thing that might happen is that he might have to run around the block before he goes to prayer meeting, but that won't hurt him much. A good response is:

159

"I am hardly driving you wild, but I will drive you home. Consider yourself gone."

There are many other lines. Men who use them run the gamut from those who know exactly what they are doing to the totally inexperienced who stumble onto a woman's weakness. Not everything a man says is sexual game playing and all men do not play the game in this manner. But many men do have ulterior motives and when sexually aroused tend to say anything to get what they want. Commitments and promises are meant at the time but later are either forgotten or denied. These men don't consider this dishonest or lying.

> *An actor is a guy who takes a girl in his arms, looks tenderly into her eyes, and tells her how great he is.*
> Great Thoughts,
> Funny Sayings

My intent here is to equip unsuspecting women with awareness, not to put down males nor produce a negative image of them. Men are great—I'm married to one! So why do men do this? Not because they are dirty old men, beasts, or party animals. Men tend to approach women sexually as part of our Creator's plan for males and females. God designed the male to be the aggressor, particularly when it comes to sex. But He does not want or expect a male to misuse this God-implanted desire. When a man's sexual drive is placed under God's control in marriage, according to His plan, it will produce positive results. This way God can always be honored.

Lines Women Use

Men certainly have no monopoly on using lines or pressuring someone for sex. In these lines from Proverbs 7:7–22, you'll see that women have done likewise since Bible times:

I saw among the simple, . . .
  young men who lacked judgment,
going down the street near her corner,
  walking in the direction of her house
  . . . as the dark of night set in.
Then out came a woman to meet him,
  dressed like a prostitute and with crafty intent.
She is loud and defiant, her feet never stay at home. . . .
  at every corner she lurks. . . .
She took hold of him and kissed him
  and with a brazen face said . . .
"I looked for you and have found you!
I have covered my bed
  with colored linens. . . .
I have perfumed my bed
  with myrrh, aloes and cinnamon.
Come let's drink deep of love till morning;
  let's enjoy ourselves with love!"
With persuasive words she led him astray;
  she seduced him with her smooth talk.
He followed her like an ox going to the slaughter.

The man mentioned in the passage is simple because he has no purpose, no goals, and doesn't know where he is going. But the adulteress knows exactly where she wants him. And she has her strategies down pat. She is dressed to allure her men (v. 10); her approach is bold (v. 13); she invites him to her place (vv. 16–18); she cunningly answers his every objection (vv. 19–20); she persuades him with smooth talk (v. 21); she traps him (v. 23). These verses outline her scheme. The strategies are clearly recognizable and as old as time itself. During this era of sexual liberation sexual pressure is very much a two-way street, and men are being openly pressured by women. Today women are less dependent on men financially and feel more in charge of their lives both in and out of the bedroom. Contraception is widely available. It is socially acceptable for a woman to seduce a man.

In the best-seller _The Burden of Proof_ a balding, pudgy, middle-aged hero was lusted after by four women. (There's hope for all you balding, pudgy, middle-aged heroes out

161

there!) The schemes of females begin long before woman-hood. Recently Ann Landers published letters from mothers whose sons were being propositioned by girls. Some twenty thousand outraged parents responded with similar stories about girls pursuing their sons. A high school guidance counselor in a small, conservative midwestern town said, "Girls seem desperate to connect and they use sex as the connection." A therapist added, "Young women who are emotionally needy but don't know how to engage the man verbally or emotionally approach him sexually."[1] The danger of such behavior is more profound than merely shocking the neighbors. Since these young women aren't emotionally ready to handle the psychological ramifications of sex, they are learning only how to relate to men sexually.

Some women in their twenties, thirties, forties, and beyond haven't moved past this level. The knowledge that they can be as forthright as they dare with a man in some carnal way is liberating. Women no longer have to pretend that they have no sexual past. A thirty-seven-year-old critical-care nurse said: "I seduced my current lover. On our first date I told him very specifically how I wanted to make love to him. It wasn't difficult to get him into bed."

From the dating and courtship seminars I've taught over the years, I've collected lines from the male population that women have used on them. They go something like this: "I thought you were a man." "You're not scared, are you?" "Maybe you're not as experienced as I thought." "Having sex is a part of nature." "If you don't, somebody else will." "I'm a virgin. You can be the first to break me in." "I want to make love to you. That's different from having sex." "You're different. I never felt toward others the way I feel toward you." "You look like you'd be good in bed."

Some men are disgusted by such sexual boldness from a woman. Peggy, an administrative assistant from San Diego, told a boyfriend she was trying to impress that on their next date she would wear a dress so tight it would look like it was spray painted on. He never called again.

Most women who are into sexual game playing don't have lines they verbalize. Instead, messages are sent nonverbally, through the way they dress or through their behavior. One woman set her sights on a recently divorced acquaintance. To let him know of her interest, she tied her bikini underwear to the antenna of his pickup. Her business card was tucked under the windshield wiper. Across it she had scrawled, "Call me." He never called.

Women Are More Vulnerable

Women are vulnerable to a man's line because, from childhood on, most women think about someone special who will hold them and love them in the way they have dreamed about. When this finally happens, a woman feels safe, protected, and loved. The moment she has waited for has arrived. This is her most vulnerable point. To keep her man, she may believe anything he says and do anything he wants. This longing to establish an intimate relationship, along with the desire for children, makes her vulnerable.

Whereas both males and females can get hurt in sexual game playing, it is the female who can be hurt the worst— through pregnancy, abortion, adoption, and the emotional trauma that follows. For a man, sex can be a physical release for urgent sexual feelings, but for a woman, it is a deeply emotional experience.

Women with low self-worth are extremely vulnerable. Mary is thirty-five and twice divorced. She works as part of a secretarial pool for a large corporation. To attract a man, she dresses provocatively and she gets dates alright, but they never get farther than the bedroom.

On an unconscious level Mary is saying to men, "I don't have much personality or other admirable qualities to offer you, but I can offer you my body." She knows she'll hate herself in the morning but she needs someone so badly tonight to take away her pain and loneliness that she'll do anything.

The root cause of Mary's behavior is low self-worth. Sex outside of marriage and low self-worth go hand-in-hand. The one who has learned to appreciate her individual worth can more easily restrain her passions. The more a person respects herself the less she needs to use sex as a means to affection. Feelings of self-worth allow a person to be patient and discriminating while progressing toward long-range goals.

Every woman needs to learn where she is vulnerable and why she acts, talks, and behaves the way she does. Knowing yourself is more important than knowing more men.

Lines and sexual game playing offer only a cheap, temporary, conditional demonstration of love. When you really care about someone you won't pressure or tempt him into doing anything he does not want to do. Love doesn't manipulate, coerce, or force. It shows respect and reaffirms the other's worth while putting what is best for the other before your own selfish desires.

Straight Talk about Body Fondling

Patty and Paul met at church where both were youth leaders. Leadership meetings threw them together and they began dating. Both had high standards and felt secure in the fact that they were Christians and members of the same church. Sexual involvement was hardly an issue for them. But one night, after watching a video at Patty's place, they went further in their hugging and kissing than either believed possible. They were so carried away, they were on the very threshold of intercourse.

Patty and Paul were brought up to believe that sex belongs exclusively in marriage. This is what they believed and their church confirmed it. But the best intentions of two committed Christians were forgotten in the heat of passion. Both were remorseful afterward. Paul promised Patty that he loved her more than ever, that he would never leave her, and that it would never happen again. "It was an accident," they rationalized. Many couples get caught like Patty and Paul did.

Chet and Paula have been going together for several months. Each has previously been married. They have been sexually active from the first date. "After all," they argue, "we're not kids anymore. Neither one of us is a virgin. We plan on getting married. We're two consenting adults and no one is getting hurt."

Marty was raised in a religious home with principles she held dear. As a single adult she began dating Andrew. He wasn't a Christian, but there were no available Christian men, so she continued to date him. He was fun, interesting, and polite but had a different agenda than Marty. They were getting into some pretty steamy episodes with him pushing hard for sex. Marty felt she could handle him. She didn't like this part of their relationship, but in order to have a male friend right now she decided to put up with it and just be careful. It wasn't long before he pushed her further than she ever dreamed anyone could prior to marriage. Pure disgust haunted her from then on.

Three stories. Three different situations. Same result.

Body fondling, what was called petting when you were a teenager, is a powerful force. People tend to make up the rules as they move along, because few know the rules. Body fondling is a step beyond hugging and kissing and yet not as far as sexual intercourse. This leaves a wide range of body-exploring activities open to question, guess, and negotiation. To clarify this dilemma, I have divided it into three stages. Stage one, a preparatory stage, includes light hugging and kissing without caressing or fondling of bodies. Stage two includes deep kissing, caressing each other's bod-

165

ies inside and outside of clothing above the waist. Stage three, a more intense and intimate stage, includes caressing each other's bodies below the waist frequently to orgasm, but without penetration.

When a man begins fondling a woman's body, he is testing the waters. How far will she let me go, he wonders. He enjoys this testing process immensely since it is sexually pleasurable and brings on sexual excitement. His mind races with anticipation as he thinks about what lies ahead. It's at this point when a man may deliver his best line: "I've never loved anyone the way I love you." His hormones are pumping and he is likely to say or do anything to get what he wants now that he is this close to satisfying his urgent sexual needs.

Her agenda is likely very different. She enjoys the hugging, holding, and kissing more than the sexual aspect. As she surrenders to his kiss and caress, her greatest emotional needs are being met. If she thinks she is in love, the affection expressed through holding fulfills her need for love and emotional security.

WAIT A MINUTE!

To engage in such intimacy outside of marriage, simply for the thrill of sexual pleasure, and to enjoy the stimulation of the moment, to make you feel good, are very selfish and self-centered indeed. Such a use of someone else's body reflects self-gratification rather than love for the other. Under such circumstances body fondling violates the principles expected to govern a relationship between a man and a woman. Particularly is this true in a casual dating relationship, when a couple is not in love and have no plans to marry each other. To engage in body fondling when not in love, cheapens a relationship. The risks are high and the rewards are low.

It's risky because body fondling caters to the temptation of taking advantage of another person. People of all ages face this temptation. At no other time is a person more vulnerable to such exploitation than when involved in body fondling. The unloved feel loved, the unattractive feel attractive, the lonely feel cared for—all under the pretense of love that may not even exist. A person's intense desire for someone else to love him can easily translate the expression of lust into a message of caring, despite the false motives.

Likewise to allow someone to hold and fondle your body outside of marriage, just to make yourself feel loved, special, and cared for is equally selfish. To allow someone access to your body to fill your temporary need to be held or to increase your feelings of worth is extremely self-serving and immature.

Let's clear something up. Body fondling is not dirty. It will not curl your toes or stunt your growth. Within the bonds of matrimony, body fondling is a beautiful experience. It is the natural expression of love called foreplay, which leads directly to sexual intercourse. What, then, is the difference between body fondling and foreplay? Many of the same activities are included but the purpose is different. Body fondling is the exploration of each other's body by two unmarried persons who should not or do not intend for intercourse to occur. And that's the trouble with body fondling. It doesn't stand alone. It moves naturally to intercourse. By itself, outside of marriage, it is more frustrating than satisfying. Our bodies were designed and created by God to respond to fondling by becoming sexually aroused and desiring intercourse. Ideally it culminates in intercourse.

When an unmarried couple engage in body fondling with the intention of not having intercourse, they must constantly be on guard to stop, lest it go too far. Body fondling, or foreplay, was not designed to stop on command. One who habitually progresses to intimate kissing and body fondling and then stops, risks the possibility of sexual malfunction in marriage. After marriage his sexual response may stop, due to the programming before marriage, and never get the message that it is okay to proceed.

167

God's plan for us is that sexual relations with our mate should be fulfilling. Starting and stopping, however, leave one very unsatisfied and frustrated. What may have been exciting before now only makes you want to go farther. This might be termed the domino theory of sex. Each time you begin body fondling, the desire accelerates, but the thrill of the particular act declines. In other words if you really enjoyed deep kissing last time, next time you'll want more.

Body fondling might be likened to crossing a bridge that spans a wide gorge. On one side is sexual intercourse and on the other side there is no physical expression of love. While body fondling you move toward the sexual intercourse side and you could be a quarter of the way across, halfway, or nine-tenths across the bridge. It's so exciting and stimulating that it's easy to find yourself across the bridge before you realize it.

Crossing the bridge doesn't always happen all at once. Sometimes it takes weeks or even months. Body fondling is dangerously progressive. Each level of excitement demands the next level. It is a powerful force for those in love who feel the sexual chemistry between them escalating.

This is particularly true for the previously married. When this person enters the dating arena, after being used to foreplay and intercourse on a regular basis, he may not know where to draw the line. Body fondling becomes dangerous and confusing, for even the most cautious of single-again individuals.

Secular philosophy tries to sell the idea that we should see how close to the edge of the cliff we can get without falling off. God would have us walk as uprightly as possible, avoiding potential danger.

Men and Sexual Arousal

Body fondling and all that goes with it affects a man differently from the way it affects a woman. Usually the two people involved do not understand what the other is experiencing. Studies have consistently shown that males and females have little or no conception of the feelings of the opposite sex. Let's look at some of the forces that entice men into sexual encounters.

Men are more sex driven than are women. The male is stimulated sexually in ways that few females realize. God made men that way, implanting in them this desire for sexual pleasure. When a male seeks to satisfy this desire, he is responding in the way God intended. He is not being dirty or evil. He is being male. This is good as long as God is always honored in the choices that are made.

Males are more visually oriented than females. Many women do not understand how their appearance affects men. Because women are not sexually aroused by merely looking at the male body or the way a man dresses, they have little realization of the effect of their appearance on men. *Psychology Today* reported the results of a study concerning clothing and behavior.[2] It found that women who wore skin-tight jeans and tight tops thought of themselves as stylish, whereas men read sexual come-ons into such dress. None of the subjects said they felt an open shirt, tight pants, tight swim trunks, or jewelry indicated that a male was on the prowl for sex. Both sexes agreed that a see-through blouse on a woman was probably a come-on, but males tended to see other clothing—low-cut tops, tight jeans, no bra, and mini skirts—as deliberately encouraging as well.

A woman does not have to wear revealing clothing to play the teasing game. She can be totally clothed and still send out signals. In fact, some women could look sexy in a sack, and a loose woman looks loose regardless of what she wears. Males can read a lot into the movements of a woman's body. If she acts loose, she'll get treated loose. The choices a woman makes in regard to her clothing and behavior become signs for men to read. She is either saying: "I respect myself and I expect you to respect me also," or "I am available to anyone interested."

Since external stimuli easily arouse a male, sex lurks close to the surface of his thinking at all times. A billboard, a dirty joke, a suggestive picture, a movie, a video, or a television program will all move him along.

Males feel a strong need to prove their masculinity. Society rears males to be strong, tough, forceful, and aggressive—capable of functioning in manly ways. Being capable sexually is one of the most important tests of masculinity. A male needs to prove to himself, and to others, that he can function like a man should. To some, sex proves this.

There are men who think the *only* proof of their manhood is having sexual relations and lots of them. The theory is that a man's masculinity relates directly to the number of females he has conquered along with an increasing number of encounters. Many times women do not understand that they are little more than a number to these men. There is a lot of laughing, joking, and crude talk about sex among this breed. Their main objective is self-gratification. Their primary concern is to enhance their own immature and shaky ego. There is no caring for the female or concern for how the encounter may affect her. Sexual gratification to this type of male is of less importance than succeeding in exerting his sexual prowess. Often these "super studs" become impotent because their misuse of sex numbs their sensitivity and they cannot integrate tender feelings with sexual feelings.

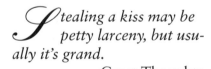

Stealing a kiss may be petty larceny, but usually it's grand.

Great Thoughts,
Funny Sayings

Studies show that men far outdistance women in the number of sex partners they have and in the number of casual sex encounters. Almost 20 percent of the men claimed twenty to forty-nine sexual partners while single. One in ten claimed to have had more than one hundred. Often this man has been divorced at least twice; is an older, upper-middle-class, playboy type; has been through a wide range of unsuccessful relationships; finds pleasure in brief relationships; is incapable of commitment; and risks very little of a personal nature in any relationship.

Dr. Stephen Levine, associate professor of psychiatry and director of the Sexual Dysfunction Clinic at Case Western Reserve University in Cleveland, describes such a man:

> A real Don Juan gets his thrill from the seduction itself—the hunt. The actual sexual experience is not that important to him, and such a man loses interest in his partner after he has been victorious. . . . They may be powerful, seductive, manipulative people who use women and generally have chaotic relationships with them.[3]

Some men try to exploit women. Devious males play at love as though it were a contest. They deliberately try to get a woman into a "touchy situation" just to see how far they can go. One study investigated sexually experienced twenty-year-old men. On the average they had already enjoyed more than three partners. Thirty-four percent had picked up women exclusively for sexual purposes or exploitative dates. They were using these women as a means to an end and reported having no feelings for the women involved. Women, no matter how sophisticated, must beware of men who take advantage of the unwary.

Women and Sexual Arousal

Men who do not really understand female arousal often assume that women are as eager for sex as they are. Actually, females respond much differently and more slowly than do males.

Due to the erection of his penis, the male is much more aware of his sexual responses than the female is of hers. His responses are more localized but her responses are more complicated. He responds more to physical factors—kissing and touching her breasts. She responds more to emo-

171

tional ones—holding, caressing, and words of love. Men can have sexual relations with women they care little for, but females tend to want strong affection to precede sexual intimacy since for them it is a deeply emotional experience. She is stimulated by the amount of romantic affection her partner has shown for her and tends to withdraw instinctively from encounters devoid of love.

So here we have a man and woman engaged in some heavy-duty sex play. He's enjoying every minute of it and secretly hopes she'll get carried away and give in to him. She's enjoying the attention but probably is not as aroused as he is. What she is enjoying, however, isn't the sexual thrill as much as the feeling of being "loved," of being cherished. Two of her major needs are being met—the need for love and for touching. Studies on female sexuality show that even those who do not achieve orgasm enjoy the sexual experience. The experience of being held and caressed is often sufficient. Someone wants her, needs her, is holding her, thinks she is attractive and sexy, and maybe even loves her. This is her most vulnerable moment.

Suddenly she wakes up to how far things have progressed. Disengaging herself, she walks away, feeling little or no discomfort. But the male is left feeling tense, physically uncomfortable, and defeated. He may repress his feelings and decide to work on her again when he can arouse her sufficiently. Each encounter weakens her defense mechanism. Most women, even sexually experienced women, have little understanding of what a man goes through when she permits intimacies but stops short of intercourse. Any woman who allows intimate kissing and caressing but who has no intention of following through is unfairly leading a man on to expect intercourse.

Because a woman's response to sexual stimuli is more gradual than a man's, it doesn't mean she doesn't enjoy it. It can be an extremely pleasurable and exciting experience, though it is not as urgent as it is for the man.

During the initial phases of foreplay, the experts agree, women respond automatically, as do men, to effective stimulation. Achieving orgasm, however, is different for the female. Tremendous emotional overtones are involved for the female that do not exist for most males. She must learn how to move toward and actively seek orgasmic release. She cannot achieve it through passivity, regardless of how skillful her partner's techniques may be. She must surrender, not only to her partner, but to her physical drive toward a climax. How can she surrender to someone she is not yet fully committed to or does not yet fully trust?

Here are some of the reasons women engage in body fondling.

Women try to satisfy their intense need for love. A primary reason women engage in intimate kissing and body fondling without intending to go further is to satisfy their God-given desire to be loved and cherished. Most women since early adolescence have dreamed of being cherished, protected, and cared for by a man. This desire continues into old age and forms the core of their emotional security. Each woman may feel in competition with every other woman for the attention of a man. The pressure is tough and she's ready to believe a man when he says, "I love you." She believes it because she wants to believe it.

When he goes on to argue that intercourse will make their love more secure, she finds his words persuasive because this is exactly what she wants to happen—not necessarily intercourse—but a lasting love relationship. Therefore women commonly color the facts to fool themselves into believing what they want to believe.

Women try to hold on to a relationship. Some women are sexually cooperative to keep a relationship going, especially if their partner has threatened to leave if they don't give in. Other women have sex so that they can have male companions. Such women stay in circulation and appear popular within a certain crowd. But listen in sometimes to what the men say about them! These relationships are based on only one thing and quickly become boring. When sex is all that keeps a relationship going, that relationship is fragile indeed. Hundreds of women have complained as this one did: "When he wants sex, he calls me, but when a nice event is scheduled, he takes someone else."

Some women try to exploit men. There are, of course, unscrupulous women who lead men on to see how far they can go. They exploit men for the sense of power they can gain over them. On a subconscious level they likely hate men, probably because their fathers neglected them during childhood. This risky game brings none of love's richness, no real satisfaction, no beauty, no permanence. Being seduced by such a woman is hardly a compliment, and a moral man will not succumb.

Caution: A man can want sex without being in love. He may interpret his strong sexual attraction as love and try to convince the woman that his love is the same as hers. She may assume that he would not ask for sex unless he loved her. She therefore gives in to his wishes feeling they have sealed a compact through intercourse. Such sexual game playing only reinforces the truth that men give love to get sex and women give sex to get love.

When all is said and done, women usually engage in intimate sexual caressing for security, not love. They feel they need to do it to get love, convey love, or to hang on to someone. But unless a couple develops something besides physical intimacies, the relationship will crumble. As someone has aptly said, "Sex can get you through the night, but what do you have that will get you through the day?" Sex alone cannot hold a marriage together. If you need intimate kissing and body fondling to build your sense of security now, later you'll need something else to help you cope with your insecurities.

10

Pair Bonding

Pathway to Intimacy

Whenever I talk with singles about the attraction between the sexes, they want to know: What's right and what's wrong before marriage? The unstated question is "How far can I go and still not sin?" Is it all right to kiss and hug? What about French kissing? Can I touch her as long as I stay above the waist and outside the clothing? Is it okay to sleep together as long as we don't have sex? Is oral sex okay?

There are many gray areas for which the Bible provides no clear-cut guidelines. But people *want* clear-cut guidelines. There is no fixed line dividing purity from sinfulness, but I have discovered research on what is called pair bonding that lays an excellent foundation for making individual decisions.

The term *pair bonding* describes the mysterious attraction between a male and a female that can develop into a love relationship. Pair bonding was first reported by secular zoologist Desmond Morris in *Intimate Behavior*. However, it was Dr. Donald Joy's book *Bonding: Relationships in the Image of God* that opened my eyes to the importance and relevance of pair bonding as a couple spend time together.[1]

The attraction between males and females encompasses far more than the physical. Included are emotional, physical, spiritual, and intellectual components. Even without the benefits of marriage, the pair become as one through time spent together, prolonged eye contact, the sharing of emotionally intimate information, and gestures of touch or caring.

Bonding is more than falling in love emotionally. It is both an emotional and physical response of two people that attaches them to each other in ways that may appear mysterious to the casual observer. Bonding describes the fusing not only of two separate and distinct individual lives, but also of their minds, ideas, and personalities. Two previously separate and distinct persons now blend their values, goals, and beliefs. Their hopes, dreams, and futures eventually merge to form one unit. Note: All of this can occur without marriage or without conscious thought.

The gift of bonding is not reserved for the young and beautiful. Whenever two persons spend time together, share feelings, and touch each other, the process of bonding is under way. The couple enter each other's world and begin to view life through another pair of eyes. As the attraction solidifies, the relationship is not easily broken.

> *Keep your eyes wide open before marriage and half shut afterwards.*
> Great Thoughts,
> Funny Sayings

If two people are separated and unable to spend time together, the developing pair bond will not necessarily be destroyed, but it may be inhibited to some degree—which is the reason long-distance romance is so difficult. The couple spend less time together than most couples and engage in less eye contact and touching.

Morris notes that the bonding process tends to be present in all human cultures as well as among animals. The twelve steps listed here were found to be consistently present in 80 percent of the five hundred cultures he studied.

Pair bonding is a gradual process, although at times it appears to happen rapidly. We simply cannot, in the true sense of the word, instantly bond ourselves to a member of the opposite sex. Initial contact may spark interest and the bonding process may be set in motion. As the relationship develops, a predictable pattern of intimacy unfolds.

Although there is no typical love relationship and each pair of lovers sees their relationship as unique, human love affairs do tend to follow a pattern.

The Twelve Steps to Pair Bonding

Stage 1: No Touch

Step 1: Eye to Body

The first glance at a person is not a sexual look but more the look of discovery. This first glance takes in size, shape, coloring, age, and personality! Immediately an almost unconscious grading process begins, rating the person on a scale of low to high interest and/or desirability. Unless the person is rated high, a second look will likely not take place. Ordinarily we would not attach great importance to step 1 and yet this step determines whether or not the relationship progresses.

Step 2: Eye to Eye

While looking each other over, the eyes occasionally meet. When this happens, there will be a quickening of the heartbeat along with the flush of embarrassment, causing a breaking of the gaze and glancing away. Usually direct eye contact is reserved for those we know and trust. So two people who are seeing each other for the first time will usually look each other over sequentially rather than simultaneously. If one likes what she sees, a smile might be added to the next

177

meeting of the eyes. Unless the eyes convey a message during future glances, the relationship will probably not proceed. Note that eye contact at step 2 is brief. At step 7 eye contact dominates.

Step 3: Voice to Voice

The next step is verbal contact. At first, the couple's conversation centers on trivia such as each other's name, where they live, what they do for a living, the weather—small talk. The exchange of small talk, however, permits further observations and analysis of tone of voice, rate of speech, accent, use of vocabulary, and mode of thinking. These all provide more information about each other.

During this stage, the couple can learn much about each other, including opinions, pastimes, hobbies, ideas, likes and dislikes, hopes, and dreams for the future. A couple should spend many hours at step 3. I, along with Dr. Joy, recommend a thousand hours at this step before progressing to step 4 when touch begins. Seemingly endless phone conversations serve a most useful purpose. Over the phone the couple is processing life together, discovering each other's inner worlds. Through all the talk on the phone, they are acquiring skills that will be critical to their relationship and possible marriage later on. Each is learning who he or she is and how to share that knowledge with the opposite sex. Each is exploring his or her inner self and becoming vulnerable, a major task when intimacy is developing. This step cannot and should not be ignored. There is much at stake. Many people advance to adulthood without developing confidence to explore their feelings with a friend. Some excel in their careers but their personal lives are a shambles. Their lack of knowledge about themselves, which should have been developed at step 3, leaves them incapable of developing emotional intimacy.

This is when the relationship needs to be slowed, before romantic gestures begin. After romantic affection begins, the couple will look at each other differently, talk about different things, and interact differently. It is during step 3 that a couple can learn if they are compatible and if the relationship should continue—all before getting romantic.

Stage 2: First Touch

During the second stage of bonding, the couple spend much time talking, but eye contact is still limited. Touch begins but none of it is directly sexual. Some light hugging and light, conventional closed-mouth kissing may take place during the next three steps. Prolonged periods of face-to-face embracing or open-mouth kissing would rush the bonding process and awaken sexual responses ahead of schedule.

Step 4: Hand to Hand

The first touch is almost always innocent and nonsexual—a handshake, accidentally touching hands while reaching for something, or touching while assisting a woman with a coat or into a car. If the woman pulls away from his touch, the man knows he cannot proceed further with such contact. If the touch is received warmly, the relationship may move into occasional and then constant hand holding, which is evidence of a growing attachment between them. Even though two hands represent only four inches of skin applied to four inches of skin, first touch along with continued touch causes a quickening of the heart and an increased indication of interest. Hand holding is also a social statement that says, "I am no longer alone. I have someone who enjoys being with me."

Step 5: Arm to Shoulder

After the thrill of holding hands begins to subside, another plateau is needed to show continued interest. Arm to shoulder touch once again increases the excitement level. While the couple is holding hands, the bodies have not been close, but the arm-to-shoulder embrace pulls the trunks of the bodies into close contact and the thrill returns. Whether the couple is seated or standing, closer body contact in the side-to-side position is maintained.

This is an easy step-up from the hand-to-hand position. The shoulder embrace is a gesture of ownership. It says more than holding hands does. In effect it states, "This relationship is going someplace." There is still limited eye contact and verbals but closer body contact.

Step 6: Arm to Waist

The excitement of holding hands and of the arm-to-shoulder embrace eventually wears thin. So to bring back the thrill, the next plateau is demanded—arm to waist. Arm to waist displays more ownership of the body. Frequently the smaller of the two will slip under the armpit of the larger, their arms crisscrossing in back. This means that often the hips are almost "glued" together.

The arm around the waist clearly signals romantic interest. A man would rarely do that to another man. Football players in a huddle may put their arms around each other's shoulders but never around the waist as it has a different connotation.

Notice that as the relationship progresses, the hands are moving down the body closer to the genitals. You may observe a couple, each wearing jeans, walking down the street in the step 6 position. Sometimes each will slip a thumb inside the back pocket for the sake of easy walking. Picture where the hand rests, directly on the buttocks. She may not be aware where her hand rests, but he knows exactly where his hand is. He is likely entertaining some interesting thoughts: If I can touch her here outside the clothing, I wonder if I might touch her inside the clothing.

Couples can frequently be observed at this stage of bonding on a school campus, at a park, standing by a car. Their bodies are close but they appear to be looking down, talking to their feet, kicking dirt, playing with something in their hands, picking grass, keeping their bodies close, and avoiding eye contact.

Deep levels of communication develop at this step. Personal disclosures are made and elaborated on. The topics for discussion are endless, but basic issues of life are being discussed and evaluated. Many personal secrets are shared and a couple really get to know each other at a deeply emotional and personal level.

Values, goals, and beliefs must be scrutinized closely. Questions that need to be answered now include: Do our life goals and personal beliefs blend well? Do we bring out the best in each other, motivating one another to better and higher challenges and accomplishments? Do we know each other's expectations for the future? Can these expectations be fulfilled? Can each allow the other to develop talents and be himself or herself? Will this person allow and encourage me to make my own decisions? boost my self-worth? Will he contribute to my happiness and well-being? Do our values regarding salvation, family life, fun, leisure time, and travel mesh? Is this person emotionally healthy? Does he have a mature understanding of life and death? Is this person capable of earning a living? Does he have a sense of belonging to a community with others? Is he free from anxiety, fears, and other emotional handicaps and from addiction to drugs? Is this person capable of developing a true friendship, free of emotional baggage from the past?

These and many other questions must be considered seriously because it is now that the future of the relationship must be made—whether it should progress or end. Enough personal disclosures have been shared so that compatibility can adequately be evaluated. If serious doubts or questions regarding any facet of the relationship exist, now is the time to say good-bye. Proceeding to step 7 or beyond and then separating can leave deep and painful scars because by then the bond is so well formed. The pain can be equal to that caused by a divorce.

Don't rush through this step. Remember that anyone can talk (some better than others, granted) but not everyone can carry on a meaningful conversation. Take time now to explore values, goals, and beliefs. Once step 7 begins it will dominate and control the relationship, allowing less time for conversing and problem solving.

Stage 3: Intimate Contact

The most significant change during stage 3 is that the couple now face one another. Although no direct sexual contact occurs, the change in body positions puts sex on a hidden agenda that both become acutely aware of. Any genital contact would bring on intercourse and could scar the formation of a healthy bond. Engaging in intercourse now would also introduce an undercurrent of mistrust and high levels of anxiety that would haunt the pair later should they marry. Communication is vastly different. Until now the couple has been developing their communication skills. Now the verbals shut down and eye contact and nonverbals take over.

Step 7: Face to Face

Three types of contact take place here: face-to-face hugging, deep kissing, and prolonged eye contact. The body position shifts from side by side to that of facing each other. Kissing now takes over and verbals shut down. It becomes obvious why compatibility and the quality of the relationship must be decided before step 7. If the couple has taken the time to talk through all the important issues of life and the foundation has been well laid, deep communication can still take place with words. Eye contact becomes long and pronounced. Verbal communication tends to shut down while the couple focus on reading each other's face.

Close body contact in this frontal position combined with open-mouth kissing and tongue thrusting bring on strong sexual arousal, particularly when repeated or prolonged. Much restraint must now be exercised by the couple since the position and activity quickly excite sexual sensitivities. Even though they are several steps away from genital contact, sexual desire has been activated and becomes a factor with which each must deal.

An unmarried couple must guard their display of physical affection carefully from this point on as all sexual motors are racing.

Step 8: Hand to Head

Here one's hand is used to caress or stroke the head of the other while kissing or talking. This intimate gesture of touch is reserved for those who have earned the right. In other words, a high level of trust has developed between the two.

Few people engage in head-touching rituals unless they are in love or are family members. This act, then, denotes emotional closeness. The sight of a lover gently running fingers through his beloved's hair or stroking the face is poignant indeed. It signals a deep bond of friendship, love, caring, and trust. The bond is well formed.

Step 9: Hand to Body

At this step the hands explore the partner's body. Breast fondling becomes an important focal point for the male. In the early stages of step 9 the fondling is outside the clothing. In the latter stage of step 9, it will move underneath the clothing but stays above the waist. Hand to body is dangerously progressive and includes back rubs, leg and feet caressing, and the like. Sexual excitement escalates and the couple experience increasing difficulty limiting the intimacy that has developed between them and not proceeding to completion of the sex act. It is now that the female usually recognizes she must call a halt or it will be too late.

Stage 4: One Flesh

Ultimate intimacy is achieved by completing the last three steps.

Step 10: Mouth to Breast

Step ten requires the baring of the female breast and is usually conducted in utmost privacy. Mouth-to-breast contact once again changes the focus of the intimacy. The couple is not only concerned with pleasure and arousal but intends to complete the sex act. Anyone progressing to step 10 would find it extremely difficult to stop short of step 12.

Step 11: Hand to Genital

The exploration of the partner's body now proceeds to the genitals. Sexual arousal and foreplay are well under way in this last most intense and intimate stage of genital fondling. Many couples stimulate each other to climax through what is commonly called mutual masturbation. Mutual masturbation involves manipulating the lover's genitals so as to attain climax without intercourse. This is done in a vain attempt to retain genital intimacy for marriage or to avoid pregnancy and sexually transmitted diseases.

Stopping at step 11 while trying to remain "pure" for marriage is faulty reasoning. The *Oxford English Dictionary* definition for the word *virgin* is "a person of either sex remaining in a state of chastity." This definition shows that at this step the line of purity has already been crossed—for both, not just the female partner. Hand-to-genital touching would hardly be considered chaste, pure, or virtuous in any culture.

The Old Testament in several places associates nakedness with illicit sexual conduct, and I suggest that when an unmarried couple caress breasts or genitals under the clothing or remove their clothing, they have gone too far. This involves body fondling in the latter stages of step 9, kissing of the breasts in step 10, and mutual masturbation in step 11. The kind of intimacy required for these three steps and especially for steps 10 and 11 is the kind of intimacy that should be reserved for marriage only. Technically it is only a breath or two away from intercourse.

After presenting the steps of pair bonding at one seminar, I received the following letter:

Dear Nancy:
I am a single woman in a steady relationship who has grown up with strong beliefs about abstinence from sex until marriage as is taught in the Bible. I have never let a man touch me below the waist although I touch them in an effort to relieve sexual pressure and make them sexually happy since I am not going to have sex until marriage. I've always prided myself on holding out and keeping myself pure till marriage but now I wonder if I really am a virgin.

Signed: Hope-to-Be-a-Virgin

Whether Hope-to-Be-a-Virgin realized it or not, by "relieving" boyfriends or masturbating them to ejaculation, she was engaging in step 11 behavior. And any couple who has proceeded this far has gone further than God would have them go in the pair-bonding process prior to marriage. One more thing bothered me in Hope-to-Be-a-Virgin's letter. Why was it acceptable for her to touch her boyfriends below the waist but not for her boyfriends to touch her below the waist? If it is wrong for males, why is it not wrong for females? I believe God spoke to Hope-to-Be-a-Virgin through her conscience, leading her to seek forgiveness and live closer to his will in the future.

Proverbs 13:19 says, "A longing fulfilled is sweet to the soul, but fools detest turning from evil." "A longing fulfilled" certainly includes stimulating sex play. Sex play is so stimulating and addictive you may lose your ability to assess it objectively. Intense desire blinds judgment and can cause you to proceed with unwise actions.

Mutual masturbation provides a great deal of sexual gratification but it has several hazards as well. Psychologists and physicians have found that the problem of many women who cannot respond freely to sexual stimulation in marriage has roots in intimate sexual encounters before marriage when their bodies became programmed to stop short of intercourse. Even after marriage, former programming still governs their response and they are unable to enjoy intercourse.

A man can be affected as well. Early negative sex experiences can result in premature ejaculation since he has become programmed to quick sex. Trauma for the male can also manifest itself in impotence, of which 90 percent is a psychological reaction to a real or imaginary experience.

Some question where oral sex fits into the pair bonding scale. It did not show up as one of the twelve steps in 80 percent of the cultures studied; therefore many cultures must have taboos against it. In oral sex the mouth provides sexual pleasure by kissing or sucking the sexual organs. This activity may, if desired, be continued to the point of orgasm.

Oral sex or any type of mouth-to-genital contact is a few degrees beyond mutual masturbation in the hierarchy of sexual experimentation. I was rapping with a large group of young men on a college campus after presenting pair bonding and was questioned about a number for oral sex. "I'd place it at eleven," I responded. A young man from the group called out, "I'd place it at twelve!" Whatever the number, a person must overcome inhibitions to expose herself to such nudity and sexual openness. I neither condemn nor condone oral sex within marriage as it is up to the couple to decide if it is right and desirable, but it should have no place during courtship.

Both mutual masturbation and oral sex require a nakedness of body and soul that should be saved for marriage only. Since both activities border on intercourse, the term "technical virginity" would apply. Only a legalistic attitude would permit the idea that because you avoid penetration you also avoid fornication.

Those who engage in oral sex also need to reckon with certain health factors. The herpes simplex virus type II causes genital herpes. The virus is passed from person to person through genital-to-genital intercourse and mouth-to-genital sex. Within a week following intimate sexual contact with someone with the herpes virus, fluid-filled blisters may develop around the sex organs or in the mouth. The sores will heal on their own within two to four weeks, but the herpes virus remains in the nerve tissue. The infected person will likely experience successive attacks of blisters and ulcers accompanied by extreme pain.

Recent research indicated that genital herpes may make women more susceptible to cancer of the cervix, although the relationship has not yet been proven. Herpes is one of several sexually transmitted diseases for which, at the time of writing, there is no cure. Medication can help suppress the symptoms and pain, but it is extremely expensive and needs to be planned into your budget.

If an expectant mother has an active infection of herpes simplex II in the vagina, her baby should be removed by Cesarean section; otherwise the infant may contract the disease while passing through the birth canal and could die.

Anyone with an active infection will of course pass it on to her sex partner. For anyone considering sex and/or marriage to a partner with herpes simplex II, remember that any time the infection is active you too will get the virus and have it for life.

Step 12: Genital to Genital

The pair-bonding process escalates to its highest level of sexual desire and is complete with penetration and sexual intercourse and in most cases orgasm. The intimacy resulting from the bond can result in pregnancy and launching of a new family life cycle, which begins with birth and bonding between parent and child.

A pair bond is thus formed by progressing through these twelve steps, culminating in sexual intercourse. But the goal should be so much more than just looking for sexual pleasure. The goal of bonding should be to develop. For a married couple, proceeding through at least the first nine steps

187

should become part of daily life in order to protect a treasured bond.[2] Moving to step 12 daily is a personal choice but daily expressions of the first nine steps are essential to keep a bond strong.

The Results of Rushing or Skipping Steps

Awareness of the developing bond while progressing through the steps sequentially and not rushing or skipping steps become essential for unmarried persons seeking to establish a strong relationship. Desmond Morris and Donald Joy both note that when the twelve-step bonding process is altered, several harmful things can happen to the potential bond formation.[3]

When steps are skipped, missed, or rushed, the bond is weakened and tends to break or become deformed. This happens because the couple did not take time to talk through the important issues—values, goals, and beliefs—prior to becoming physically involved. Once the sexual motors get turned on, people tend to forget other aspects of relationship building. It is easier and faster to get to know each other physically than emotionally, socially, and spiritually.

Does the couple recognize they are forming an imperfect bond during the process? Of course not! They are having too much fun indulging in sexual intimacies. Every nerve in their body is pulsating sexual vigor. When do they wake up to the fact that sexual excitement can't hold things together forever? After they've been married for a while. That's when she looks at him and says, "You never talk to me." And he says, "You don't understand me." Neither one has ever communicated with or understood the other but they never took the time to find that out. Once the sexual motors were turned on, they failed to check out other areas of the relationship. The process of building a relationship that lasts a lifetime must be slowed during the first six steps, during the communication process, or there is a high probability of a weak marriage.

After a couple break up, the tendency is to accelerate the steps with the next partner. For example, Dick and Jane frequently engage in light and sometimes intense body fondling (step 9). Although they have not yet proceeded to intercourse, they have become accustomed to this level of sexual arousal. Within a few weeks Dick loses interest in Jane and begins dating Sally. Immediately he attempts to move Sally to step 9 since he is used to this level of excitement.

Jane moves into a new relationship with Ralph. Ralph is sexually inexperienced and wants to take his time getting to know Jane. Jane feels he doesn't care much for her when he only holds her hand (step 4) and attempts no sexual liberties. She then encourages and actually pushes him to step 7 and beyond. Neither Dick nor Jane takes time in the next relationship to get to know the partner as they should. Steps are rushed and sometimes skipped entirely. Should they marry later on, they will likely find themselves in a very troubled relationship, never fully understanding why until it is too late.

Every progression of physical affection establishes a new plateau, making it extremely difficult to retreat once it has been reached. Each level of sexual excitement is so immediately rewarding it becomes nearly impossible to again be satisfied with lower levels. Each step in the pair-bonding process then must be carefully thought through and chosen. Such thinking runs contrary to the popular "if-it-feels-good-do-it" philosophy. The long-term consequence of uninhibited sexual freedom is difficulty settling down to one partner after multiple matings.

A sexually experienced person will tend to rush a new partner to intercourse. This tracks the previous point. A person who is used to proceeding through all twelve steps of sexual arousal without stopping will find it difficult to slow the process or to stop at steps 7, 8, or 9. This presents a real problem for any sexually experienced person as well as the formerly married. Formerly married persons are not accustomed to stopping. Sexual intercourse has been achieved without thinking through levels or steps. When a marriage ends and this person returns to the dating scene, pair-bonding steps become a blur. Many start dating and immediately become sexually involved, thinking it is just the normal thing to do. For such persons years have elapsed since they have been part of the single scene and had to think through sexual issues— what's right and what's wrong or how far to go. For someone who is carrying painful or emotional baggage from either the death of a spouse or from a divorce, the excitement of being with someone who finds her sexually desirable may be overwhelming. Without thinking through the consequences of rapidly building a new relationship, this person may slide into sexual involvement with only a twinge of conscience. *After all,* she reasons, *everybody is doing it. We're two consenting adults.* Rushing to sexual intimacy before marriage is one good explanation for the higher divorce rate in second and third marriages.

Dr. Donald Joy confirms this thought. He believes defective pair bonding is the real culprit in the rate of divorce in our culture.

> . . . anthropologists faithfully report that our high premium on so-called social experience is contributing to patterns of promiscuity and its defective bonding. Our divorce statistics are likely more related to the amount of unprotected pair bonding—and to social pressure to be sexually active before marriage—than to any other one cause.[4]

We all want guidelines for our relationships. But we either haven't known what the guidelines are or we've been afraid to state them regarding what intimacies are appropriate for differing types of relationships. The Puritans of New England had specific guidelines. They practiced "bundling"— putting a couple in love in bed together in a private room.

A board down the length of the bed separated them. They were told they could talk, touch, feel, but no more. There was a line they could not and should not cross. Once the steps to pair bonding are understood, we too can acknowledge the realities of sexual pressure and set up appropriate guidelines.

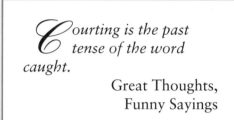

Courting is the past tense of the word caught.

Great Thoughts,
Funny Sayings

The consequences of rushing, skipping, or missing steps apply every bit as much to middle-aged and older adults as to young adults. Many singles, after divorce or the death of a spouse, reenter the dating scene acting much like adolescents in love, unable to keep their hands off each other. Within a short time after marriage they too act like so many other married people—the dreary monotony of unfulfilled dreams takes over, the light is gone from their eyes and there is no more touching. How did this happen? By rushing the pair-bonding steps, they never really got to know the person they married until it was too late. In fact the formerly married are more likely to rush the pair-bonding steps because of their past experience in marriage. Everyone, whether married or single, must bring sexual desire under God's control, minute by minute submitting choices to Him to avoid a life of heartache.

Now that the twelve pair-bonding steps have been outlined we can better determine what demonstration of physical affection is appropriate for each stage of dating. Your values committed to God, along with how much you value yourself, dictate your choices. As you map out your intentions for your current relationship and for all future relationships, remember that everyone crossing the boundary from step 6 to step 7 risks exposing herself to the same trauma that follows a divorce due to the intense bond that is formed.

In my estimation steps 9–12 belong in marriage only and have no place in a relationship prior to the wedding ceremony.

An Invitation to Sexual Purity

The Bible addresses the subject of sex openly. In Scripture sex is neither dirty nor the ultimate experience. God's Word clearly states, however, that sexual intercourse is reserved only for those who have entered the state of marriage.

Some feel exempted from God's Word, if they are not promiscuous, and they suffer no remorse or guilt regarding their past. When we disobey the laws of health, we will at some point suffer the consequences of our choices. In like manner, violation of God's law regarding sexual purity produces a harvest of devastating consequences, although we may not be aware of them immediately.

God's plan for our lives is perfect and has never changed. Sexual intimacy for marrieds is God's special design for procreation and for our enjoyment and it is part of pair bonding. This is the only lifestyle that offers complete happiness.

In the eyes of the world, the choice to remain sexually pure prior to marriage may seem unrealistic and Victorian, but the facts supporting such a choice remain in your favor. Your sexuality might be considered a gift from God marked, "For greatest enjoyment, do not open till married."

Whenever a relationship is based on physical pleasure rather than friendship it will eventually burn itself out. It's the qualities found in friendship that will get you through the days and also through a lifetime bonded to one person.

At one time Christ walked this earth. Scripture records that "[he was] tempted in every way, just as we are—yet was without sin" (Heb. 4:15). This means that He faced sexual temptation. Yet He did not falter, toy with the idea, or give in. In the face of temptation He was able to turn away and remain pure. His life serves as an example for us today. "Let us then approach the throne of grace with confidence, so that we may receive mercy and find grace to help us in our time of need" (Heb. 4:16).

If you commit your life to Jesus, you can rest assured that He can and will control your sex life when you ask for guidance. He will provide the strength to resist temptation. You do not have to battle your urges on your own. He will guide in this area of your life. Specifics on how to harness sexual desire and bring it under God's control will be addressed in the next chapter. It is possible to slow the pair-bonding instinct and make wise choices that will lead to a life of purity.

11

Abstinence

O ur God is a God of freedom. He has given us the freedom to make choices that determine the direction of our life. But our God, in addition to being a God of choices and freedom, also says, "I have something for you that is better than temporary pleasure. Follow Me. Wait on Me. Deny yourselves just a small portion of the pleasure available today and I will give you permanent joy, peace, and a lifetime of companionship with Me."

Many of us can't wait to experience what God has to offer. We may have sunk so low we no longer have hope for the future. We reject God's offer because we can't see or experience the joy right now. The loss to us and to our families now and throughout eternity is incalculable.

Evidence on Abstinence

For years I've been collecting data on why it is wiser to wait until marriage for sex. Sociological, psychological, and medical evidence all support an abstinence stand. The possible outcomes of sex outside of marriage are extremely dangerous. It destroys family life as well as the purpose and meaning of marriage. It erodes a person's ability to love and turns people into objects, which degrades their self-worth. It can lead to disease and result in unwanted children.

Furthermore, sex outside of marriage is a sin against God. The Bible is clear on the subject. In the King James Version of the New Testament the word *fornication* refers to sexual immorality in general (John 8:41; Acts 15:20, 29; 21:25; Rom. 1:29; 1 Cor. 6:13, 18; 2 Cor. 12:21; Eph. 5:3). Two passages (Matt. 5:32; 19:9) use *fornication* as a synonym for adultery. In four passages both *adultery* and *fornication* are used together, indicating a definite distinction between the two words (Matt. 15:19; Mark 7:21; 1 Cor. 6:9; Gal. 5:19). Two references refer to voluntary sexual intercourse between unmarried people or between an unmarried person and a married person (1 Cor. 7:2; 1 Thess. 4:3–5). In 1 Corinthians 5:1 Paul applies the word *fornication* to an incestuous relationship.

In the final analysis then, thirty-seven out of thirty-nine biblical passages exclude premarital sexual intercourse from God's plan for men and women. The two exceptions are where fornication is used as a synonym for adultery. God asks His children to confine sexual intercourse to marriage. The biblical injunction is simple, clear, and straightforward.

Many singles understand on an intellectual level that Scripture prohibits premarital sex but they often believe that those prohibitions were only for the time of the early church. Today things are different. Guidelines regarding sex outside of marriage have changed, they feel. We're more sophisticated now. God had His reasons for telling the children of Israel to remain celibate outside of marriage. But such regulations are archaic.

I stress total abstinence—sexual purity—until marriage. But preaching abstinence is sometimes like spitting into the wind. Not because singles won't listen. They try to listen, but abstinence messages often get drowned out by the entertainment industry's steamy sex dramas and its safe-sex propaganda.

God didn't make rules to see how good we are at jumping through hoops or scoring points. The purpose of His laws is to protect us, because He knows they are in our best interest. If we follow them, we will live longer, happier, and more fulfilling lives—we will prosper. This is true even though His laws may not make sense to us now.

Some argue that it is all right to break God's law against sexual sin if nobody gets hurt. In truth, somebody always gets hurt. Even if you escape disease and pregnancy, the ability to commit or to bond with one person for a lifetime is scarred as well as the ability to trust, to feel sexual desire, and to be fully open with another person. God's laws are not arbitrary. They do not forbid sexual pleasure; rather they preserve sexual pleasure if we abide by them and keep sexual intimacy for marriage.

Sin has the power to hurt and ultimately destroy us. That's what disobedience will do in the end—destroy.

It's foolish to tempt God, to wait and see what will happen. The best time to learn the dangers of going after forbidden sex is long before temptation occurs. Resistance is easier when you've already decided that you don't want to indulge in premarital sex.

Fifteen Benefits of Total Abstinence

There are a multitude of benefits to total and complete abstinence before marriage. I've narrowed my list to fifteen. Do not assume because one precedes another, it carries more weight. They are not given in order of importance.

1. *Abstinence before marriage helps prevent divorce.* Women who are sexually active before marriage are more likely to divorce than those who abstain. Joan Kahn and Kathryn London studied 2,746 women in the National Sur-

vey of Family Growth and measured the odds. The study, conducted over a twenty-year period, reported in a recent issue of the _Journal of Marriage and the Family_ that virgin brides were less likely to end their marriage through divorce or separation than women who had not been virgins at marriage. How much less likely? The results are astonishing. Nonvirgins have a divorce rate 53 percent to 71 percent higher than do virgins.[1]

Drs. Kahn and London elaborate on these statistics. Virgin women are more likely to be religious and brought up in strict homes. This unprecedented sociological evidence proves that those who embrace and practice biblical standards can increase their odds of a lasting marriage. Conversely, those who are not virgins at the time of marriage increase their odds of divorce by 60 percent.

2. _Abstinence before marriage helps prevent unnecessary breakups._ Studies show that couples who engage in sex before marriage are more likely to break up than those who do not. Even formally engaged couples who have intercourse are more likely to break their engagements. Why? One reason is that sex drives are being satisfied before marriage. (For more information on this subject, see my book _The Compleat Courtship._)

The biological force of sex attracted the two; once that force is relieved, the power that drew them together declines. Part of the sexual attraction between male and female is the desire to understand the mystery about the other. Once the "ultimate" has been done, there is little curiosity left. In time the relationship levels off rather than deepening as the couple imagined it would. Interest in sex is not lost. The couple continue their sexual pattern but sense its decline. And when a breakup occurs, it is far more painful—because of the bonding that has taken place—than if they had never entered a sexual liaison.

3. _Abstinence before marriage prevents much sexual dysfunction for the female._ Some studies indicate half of all

197

American wives have such poor attitudes about sex they cannot achieve orgasm. Women (as well as men) tend to harbor guilt and fear about past performances with previous partners. When this happens, poor habits and attitudes adopted outside marriage rob them of full sexual enjoyment.

In studies conducted on women who have had sexual intercourse prior to marriage, it was found that the more premarital sexual experience women have had prior to marriage, the more likely they are to experience orgasm during intercourse in the first year of marriage. This held true for those who had sexual relations only with their future husband as well as for those having several partners.

If we stopped here, it would appear that abstinence doesn't pay. But despite their ability to reach orgasm, far more of these women had sex difficulties during the early days of marriage. Significant numbers reported long-term difficulties and dysfunction that began during the first two weeks of marriage. Others reported feeling like "sex servants."

Different dynamics take over after marriage. Women who freely indulged boyfriends before marriage confronted an array of emotions and difficulties after marriage that they had been unaware of just weeks before. And the more devout the woman, the greater the likelihood of her experiencing regret and guilt.

Women without previous sexual experience are quick to learn how to achieve orgasm after marriage. The American Institute of Family Relations questioned two thousand married women regarding their orgasmic response. Twenty-eight percent of the women who were virgins on their wedding day experienced orgasm, compared with 39 percent of those with sexual experience prior to marriage. These differences disappeared quickly with experience during marriage. By the end of the first year, virgin wives equaled nonvirgin wives in response.

Whether or not a woman is able to achieve orgasm seems to be connected to guilt. When sin is indulged in repeat-

198

edly—in this case, sex outside of marriage—guilt is the natural outcome. Fear and loss of self-respect for not following moral codes and religious values follow. As remorse is felt and compounded with each indulgence, negative feelings become associated with the sex act. Such feelings do not disappear even after the marriage ceremony takes place.

4. _Abstinence before marriage prevents much sexual dysfunction for the male._ Impotence, the inability to maintain an erection, affects about one out of ten males and is caused by a variety of both physical and emotional factors. Anger, fear, resentment, and guilt can cause impotence. Ego or self-worth problems in which masculinity is threatened, including fear of rejection, can also be contributing factors.

One man who experienced impotency during the first year of marriage said, "My sex drive was greater while we were living together than now." Another man admitted to his first bout with impotency after he and his girlfriend were "caught in the act" by her parents. A third man who began having intercourse with his fiancée just weeks before the wedding told his pastor, "I go limp every time we go to bed, and my wife can't take it." The common denominator in each of these cases? Sex before marriage.

Another problem for males is premature ejaculation and can result from poor sex habits prior to marriage. A man suffering from this condition cannot withhold ejaculation long enough to bring a woman to climax at least 50 percent of the time. This problem plagues younger more than older men and may be traced to a variety of scenarios: frequent sex play when the man became used to ejaculating without vaginal penetration, a rendezvous where "getting caught" was feared, or sex in a pay-as-you-go encounter. One's sexual nature is forever hooked up with the psychological nature. Sex cannot be isolated or compartmentalized, separated from other aspects of life. How someone conducts his sex life will affect his mental and psychological processes as well. Abstinence before marriage protects from negative effects on the psyche.

5. *Abstinence prior to marriage assists in the prevention of cervical cancer.* Young women who engage in sex with multiple partners are at a high risk of contracting cervical cancer when they are forty to forty-five years old. About the time menstruation begins, the entire endocrine system is stabilized. Finishing touches are put on the uterus, fallopian tubes, and ovaries. The cervix is extremely vulnerable during this time. If exposed to semen, from one or multiple partners, a woman is placed at risk for cancer of the cervix in later life. Semen contains so-called "antigens" that sensitize or code the cervix and may cause abnormal development when a woman is exposed to it too early, too often, and by multiple sex partners. When a woman has three or more sexual partners she is fifteen times more likely to get cervical cancer than a woman who has only one partner.[2]

6. *Abstinence prior to marriage eliminates the risk of contracting a sexually transmitted disease (STD).* If you are having sex outside the exclusive marriage bed, you are a prime candidate for STDs. Unmarried partners simply do not know one another's sexual histories. Studies reveal that such persons are very uncomfortable discussing STDs, contraception, or condom use and think they can sense or know when a partner is or isn't safe. No one can intuitively know. One study showed that 20 percent of the men—but just 4 percent of the women—said they would not tell a potential partner they had tested positive for HIV. Forty-seven percent of the men and 42 percent of the women said they would understate the number of previous sex partners.[3] In a new national survey men reported an average of fifteen sex partners; women reported eight.[4]

Women are more vulnerable to AIDS than men because the vagina is highly susceptible to cuts or tearing during intercourse. Another reason women are at higher risk is because the virus is more concentrated in semen than in vaginal fluid and susceptible cells of the vagina are exposed to the semen for a prolonged period of time.[5]

Safe sex isn't safe. The failure rate in preventing pregnancy for couples using condoms is at least 15.7 percent of the time annually. Among young unmarried minority women the failure rate for preventing pregnancy is 36.3 percent annually. The *British Medical Journal* reports the failure rate in preventing pregnancy due to slippage and tearing of the condom to be 26 percent. Obviously anyone who relies on condoms for birth control can be called a parent! This super high failure rate exists in preventing pregnancy—where a woman can conceive only one to two days per month. We can only guess the failure rate for preventing STDs, which can be transmitted 365 days per year!

> *Like the bee sting, the promiscuous leave behind them in each encounter something of themselves by which they are made to suffer.*
>
> Great Thoughts,
> Funny Sayings

Condoms cannot be accurately tested for AIDS protection. The AIDS virus is 450 times smaller than sperm and can easily pass through the smallest detectable hole.

Now get this: If you have had two to three sex partners and your partner has had two to three sex partners, you have a 100 percent chance of getting an STD. To help you understand this, look at Peter and Paula, who have been going together and are considering becoming sexually involved. Both know the other has had previous partners but neither has been specific nor truthful. Let's look at the whole picture. (See the following diagram.[6]) Peter's former girlfriend is Diane. Peter and Diane had sex. Diane had sex with two other men, Chuck and Jon, before she had sex with Peter. Chuck's three partners before Diane were Patti, Deanna, and Judy. Deanna had sex with one person, Jason, before Chuck. Jason's former partner was Janet. Judy's first partner was Scott. Jon's former girlfriend was Betty. Betty had two previous sexual relationships, with Tom and with Kevin. Kevin was bisexual and involved with Jack.

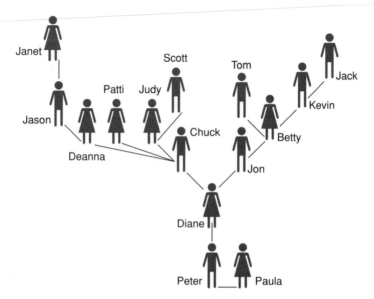

Adapted from *Risky Times* by Jeanne Blake. Used by permission of Workman Publishing Co., Inc.

So if Paula thinks she is safe with Peter, she is forgetting about the other thirteen people in the picture. Former U.S. Surgeon General C. Everett Koop said that when you sleep with a person, in essence you sleep with all his or her previous sex partners.

Here is a progression worked out, assuming all partners have the same history—one partner per year, beginning at age 30. At the end of the year you would have had sex with one person. At age 31, 3 persons—last year's partner, your current partner, and the person your current partner had sex with last year. At age 32, 7 persons. At age 33, 15 persons. At age 34, 31. At age 35, 63 persons. At age 36, 127. One hundred and twenty-seven is a conservative assumption, since it is not uncommon for first sexual encounters to begin at age fifteen, not age thirty. The cumulative effect builds yearly.

It is possible to be a carrier of an STD like AIDS for fifteen years and not know it. The only way to be sure you will not get an STD is to be in a monogamous relationship with someone who is also monogamous. Otherwise you must examine not only your current sex partner but all of your partner's partners for the last fifteen years.

7. *Abstinence before marriage predicts greater sexual satisfaction after marriage.* A recent study by the Family Research Council titled "What's Marriage Got to Do with It?" found that 72 percent of all married traditionalists (those who strongly believe out-of-wedlock sex is wrong) report high sexual satisfaction—roughly 31 percentage points higher than the level registered by unmarried nontraditionalists![7]

Joseph and Mary Ann Mayo, coauthors of a book on the subject, say: "It was those with the least sexual experience who were more likely to report their marriage as 'always warm and supportive.'"[8]

According to nationally syndicated columnist Michael McManus, author of the book *Marriage Savers*, if a couple abstain from sex prior to marriage, they are 29 to 47 percent more likely to enjoy sex after marriage.[9]

A recent survey on sexuality by *U.S. News and World Report*, dubbed the "most authoritative ever," sheds further light on the subject. This survey, conducted jointly by researchers at State University of New York at Stony Brook and the University of Chicago, found that of all sexually active people, those who reported being most physically pleased and emotionally satisfied were the married couples.

A chance at this kind of sexual enjoyment alone would make it all worth waiting for!

8. *Abstinence prior to marriage insures a more perfect bond.* It is impossible to predict prior to having intercourse with someone what your attitudes or the attitudes of your

partner will be following the experience. Sex changes the dynamics of the relationship. There are innumerable ramifications of sexual intercourse, ramifications that cannot be altered. You may look at yourself, the other person, and life through different eyes.

For instance, as a result of intercourse a woman frequently feels a strong attachment to the man—an emotional bond that cannot be forgotten years later even though she may have married someone else. Or the woman who submits reluctantly may begin to think of sex as a commercial enterprise existing as a masculine prerogative. Other people feel used, dirty, and ashamed because something has been lost that can never be reclaimed. Still others suffer from intense confusion and bewilderment.

It isn't just a matter of whether or not you engage in sex prior to marriage, but how often and with how many partners. If you have sex with only one person before marriage, all the consequences will apply, but the toll will be infinitely greater when multiple partners are involved.

9. *Abstinence prior to marriage decreases the likelihood of extramarital affairs.* A strong positive correlation exists between sex before marriage, even when limited to one partner, and extramarital sex. Studies relating premarital to extramarital sex show that those who have had premarital sexual experience are twice as likely to have extramarital affairs as those who are virgins at marriage. Furthermore, a greater proportion of those who have had extramarital affairs think they will do so again. This strong correlation between premarital and extramarital sex can also be used to predict unhappiness in marriage and a likelihood of divorce.[10]

People who have had a variety of come-and-go lovers find it difficult to do an about-face at their wedding and commit themselves to a lifetime of fidelity within the sacred bonds of matrimony. Sexual appetites established before marriage strongly affect and direct sexual appetites after marriage.

10. *Abstinence before marriage improves chances of distinguishing real love from infatuation.* It is difficult enough to distinguish real love from infatuation even as a mature adult, and when sex is part of the relationship it distorts true feelings. In most instances, the longer a couple goes together, the greater their chance of finding true love; but when a couple becomes sexually involved, they may stay together for the sex, not because they share common interests, goals, and values. A woman may continue a sexual relationship so she can keep her man. He stays with her for enjoyable sex.

A couple begin dating. As their relationship progresses their compatibility is tested. When mostly compatible, they stay together. When incompatible, they break up. This is the way it works when a couple is not sexually involved. But as soon as a relationship becomes sexual, the dynamics change, whether either will admit it or not.

Sex before marriage inevitably masks areas of concern that should be discussed as a relationship moves along. Often, when a sexually active couple encounter a problem, rather than dealing openly with it, the problem is masked by having sex, which seems to make things better temporarily. Thus the couple never develop critical problem-solving skills. On the surface everything progresses well, but they never learn to communicate. The sexual involvement may mask difficulties until after marriage.

When sex begins before a couple learns vital communication skills, it invariably becomes manipulative. Studies indicate that a sexual relationship may hold a couple together for three to five years, but no longer.

Abstinence can help a couple learn to communicate and problem solve when they are committed to spending time learning critical communication skills.

11. *Abstinence before marriage eliminates guilt feelings.* Women generally feel more guilt when breaking their moral code than do men, but men also experience regret as a result of promiscuous behavior prior to marriage.

To the extent that a person associates sex before marriage with guilt, shame, and fear, to that same degree that person will experience the same devastating emotions after marriage. Such attitudes or emotions may take months or even years of professional counseling to eradicate.

There is difficulty in predicting when guilt will surface. It may be experienced immediately following a sexual encounter or later as regrets gnaw at the conscience. Ernest Hemingway supposedly once commented that *moral* is what you feel good after; *immoral* is what you feel bad after. Hemingway's statement could be a guideline for life if you are living only for the moment, but if you want to do now what will be good for you ten years from now, you need a higher standard. It is difficult for a lonely or love-starved person to make a wise choice about what will make him happy ten or twenty years hence. The conscience is not a totally reliable guide. It can be duped, especially in the heat of passion. That is why many people continue in premarital sexual relations and don't feel guilty about it.

12. *Abstinence promotes self-worth.* Repeated indulgence in known wrong destroys self-worth. In his book *No Wonder They Call Him the Savior,* Max Lucado relates a story that originally appeared in the *Miami Herald.*

> Judith Bucknell was homicide number 106 that year. She was killed on a steamy June 9 evening. Age: 38. Weight: 109 pounds. Stabbed seven times. Strangled. She kept a diary. Had she not kept this diary perhaps the memory of her would have been buried with her body. But the diary exists as a painful epitaph to a lonely life. The correspondent made this comment about her writings: "In her diaries Judy created a character and a voice. The character is herself, wistful, struggling, weary; the voice is yearning. Judith Bucknell has failed to connect; age 38, many lovers, much love offered, none returned."
>
> Successful as a secretary, but a loser at love. Her diary was replete with entries such as the following: "Where are the men with the flowers . . . and music? Where are the men

who call and ask for a genuine, actual date? Where are the men who would like to share more than my bed, my booze, my food? . . . I would like to have in my life, once before I pass through my life, the kind of sexual relationship which is part of a loving relationship."

She never did. Judy was not a prostitute. She was not on drugs or on welfare. She never went to jail. She was not a social outcast. She was respectable. She jogged. She hosted parties. She wore designer clothes and had an apartment that overlooked the bay. And she was very lonely. "I saw people together, and I'm so jealous I want to throw up. What about me? What about me?"

Though she had many lovers (59 in 56 months), she had little love. "Who is going to love Judy Bucknell?" the diary continues. "I feel so old. Unloved. Unwanted. Abandoned. Used up. I want to cry and sleep forever."[11]

Old . . . unloved . . . unwanted . . . abandoned . . . used up . . . cry . . . sleep forever. These are hardly words of wisdom from someone who has discovered the secret of happiness.

Women frequently engage in sex for nonsexual reasons. A woman goes out with a man and then to bed with him, not because she wants to or loves him but because she feels it is expected of her. She suspects that unless she plays the game his way, she'll not hear from him again. Engaging in sex because she thinks it's part of some unspoken deal eventually makes a woman feel guilty and used. Guilt and feeling used lead to increased feelings of self-hate.

Even men admit that a one-night stand isn't as great as it's made out to be. Dr. Joyce Brothers says: "Instant sex is about as satisfying as a sneeze, without a loving relationship."

Sex is not the answer to feeling unloved, unwanted, abandoned, and used. Judith Bucknell sacrificed her self-worth at the altar of sex. Sex outside of marriage only complicates the problems we already have. The answers to such problems can be found when we have a committed relationship to Jesus Christ.

> *I want to tell you a terrific story about oral contraception. I asked a girl to sleep with me and she said no.*
>
> Great Thoughts,
> Funny Sayings

13. *Abstinence before marriage totally eliminates the risk of pregnancy.*

14. *Abstinence prior to marriage precludes the need of abortion.* Though we don't read about it in the media, women in their forties have a rate of unwanted pregnancy that equals that of teenagers.[12] And many mature adult women solve their problem by having an abortion.

Millions of women suffer intensely following an abortion. Physically, they suffer from nervous disorders and stomach problems; and some, because of complications, have to have hysterectomies, which preclude their ever giving birth to another child. Mentally, they suffer from depression, feelings of rejection, guilt, suicidal thoughts, and an inability to forgive themselves.

Yes, abortion has an aftermath that until recently has been ignored. One study by Dr. Anne Catherine Speckhard at the University of Minnesota included women from diverse backgrounds who endured surprisingly similar symptoms:

- 81 percent reported preoccupation with the aborted child
- 73 percent reported flashbacks of the abortion
- 69 percent reported feelings of craziness after the abortion
- 54 percent reported recurring nightmares related to the abortion
- 35 percent perceived visitations from the aborted child
- 23 percent suffered hallucinations related to the abortion[13]

These symptoms occurred in spite of the fact that 72 percent said they held no religious beliefs at the time of their abortion! We can only imagine the repercussions on the mother, as well as the father of the child, who were raised Christians and broke their code of values in seeking abortion as the answer to a difficult dilemma.

Any woman who has had an abortion needs to seek repentance, healing, and the assurance of Christ's forgiveness and overwhelming mercy. Once she truly understands Christ's mercy and forgiveness, she can let go of the guilt and hurt. It takes time to heal and the process of forgiving oneself cannot be hurried. A woman may not experience the manifestations of post-abortion trauma for five to ten years after the abortion. Therefore women go on to marry unsuspecting mates and do not recognize the root cause of problems that may surface years later.

15. *Abstinence preserves the value and meaning of the honeymoon.* The lingering memories of a happy and special honeymoon bless a couple for many years. As married life progresses, a couple should be able to look back on their honeymoon as a choice memory. One study indicated that 87 percent of the couples who had practiced abstinence until marriage had a honeymoon, as compared with only 47 percent of couples who had been sexually intimate prior to marriage.[14] One recently married male said: "Having sex before we were married greatly took away my expectations for our honeymoon. After we were married, I was truly sorry I'd let it happen, but it was too late."

Not having sex outside of marriage. It's called abstinence. And it's 100 percent guaranteed to work. You won't get hurt, get an STD, get pregnant, or suffer a host of other ills. You can choose abstinence any time, even when you've previously been sexually active.

Abstinence. It works! And it pays great dividends.

12

God's Plan for Sex

A prominent marriage counselor once said, "The only sound motive for a happy marriage is being overwhelmingly in love on a frankly sexual basis, centering about physical desire." Now if he had stopped there, many could build a case for whatever they might want to condone. But he went on to add that, fundamental though sex is, "there is much more to a good marriage."

Sex by itself is little more than animal appetite. Genuine love combines sexual desire with other components that build the highest kind of relationship between husband and wife. Love is friendship, tenderness, self-control, selflessness, kindness, and loyalty blended with sexual desire.

The sexual urge, separated from other aspects of a relationship, selfishly desires to dominate, conquer, force, or surrender. By itself it is animal. Genuine love idealizes, controls, and conforms sexual desire to social living. Love is other-person centered. Sex without love is self-centered, a craving for physical satisfaction, physical release. Love, on the other hand, craves an intimate sharing with another person.

The Ten Key Habits of Sexually Abstinent People

To you who made a decision to remain celibate until marriage and stuck to it, I salute you. You have chosen a better, safer route. It has probably been a lonely road. Hollywood and the media have contempt for you. Many lost, confused, sick people mock and resent you.

To you who feel trapped by sexual sin, I offer hope. Are you trying to convince yourself how great sex is when in reality it leaves you empty and lonely? Then take a long hard look at the real you. Be ruthlessly honest. Is your life a plus or a minus? Picture yourself ten years from now. If you continue your present course of behavior, will you be where you really want to be?

Let's say you'd like to make some changes. In today's sex-saturated society, can a sexually experienced adult who possesses a very real sex drive and is perhaps very much attracted to a member of the opposite sex put on the brakes? By the time you become sexually attracted to someone, and especially if you have fallen in love, advice falls on deaf ears. As one basketball coach quipped, "As long as my team is winning I can't teach them anything."

If you've been celibate and want to stay that way until marriage, here's how to maintain your choice. And for the sexually experienced, here are ten surefire strategies to integrate abstinence into your future.

1. *Develop positive feelings of worth.* Having positive feelings about yourself is the most important factor in avoiding sexual involvement prior to marriage. If you live up to your values, others will think highly of you, and inner conflicts will not tear you up inside. You will respond to others' opinions of you with personal integrity and self-confidence. Your appearance, abilities, or social acceptance will not unduly worry you and this leaves you freer to love, work, and play.

211

A. C. Green, one of the great all-star basketball players, says that as a professional athlete he is constantly confronted by women who want to meet and spend time with him. From the time he arrives in a city until he leaves, women pursue him. Professional basketball players often have a larger-than-life image, and such women are everywhere, he says—in the airports, hotel lobbies, restaurants, and sports arenas—trying to catch his eye.

A. C. isn't blind. He recognizes the kind when he sees one. Furthermore he hears the locker-room talk about the sexual conquests of other players. Yet he has chosen to remain sexually pure until marriage, to follow God's standards rather than secular standards. This has been verbalized to his teammates. He has told them what his stand on sex before marriage is and that he believes God has reserved sex for marriage. His teammates don't all agree with his stand but they respect him for taking it and standing up for it. A. C. is proud to be a virgin. "I have to respect myself before I can respect others," he says. Right on, A. C.!

If you are going to practice abstinence from this day forward, you must first improve your feelings of worth. (See chapters 1 and 2 on how to do this.) When you truly see yourself as a valued child of God for whom Christ died, you will feel more capable of making hard choices that will benefit your future instead of weakening it.

2. *Set rules for your conduct in advance.* Most singles have never set limits on their conduct, not even their sexual conduct. Phrases like "I never really thought about it" or "I play it by ear" or "I wait and see" are commonly used. Such "go-with-the-flow" attitudes create opportunities for pressure situations to develop.

You must think through your standards and develop criteria for physical intimacy based on your personal values and God's Word. Take time for a thoughtful self-inventory and decide what limits you will put on your behavior. Decide at what point in the steps to pair bonding you will stop in any relationship with the opposite sex until you are married. Call up in your mind the number of the pair-bonding step. This should be a point you would be proud to discuss with your pastor or a trusted friend.

After carefully thinking through and setting your standards, plan how to maintain them. Develop a specific plan to follow so that you can continue in a healthy, growing love relationship with a member of the opposite sex without compromising yourself (you can use the following eight habits to help develop your plan).

Babe Ruth once played before a hostile stadium. Amid the boos and hissing, he pointed his bat to the exact spot in the grandstand where he intended to hit the next pitch. Then he hit the ball to precisely where he had pointed—for a home run. When you are setting up rules for your conduct, think of Babe Ruth. Everyone else might say you'll never make it, but your standards can never be too high. The more clearly your standards are defined and the better you know yourself and your standards, the more likely you are to achieve them. Just keep thinking about where the bat is pointed.

A quotation that I heard once sums up some of the best advice I ever heard: "It's a funny thing about life. If you refuse to accept anything but the best, you very often get it."

3. _Talk it over with your dating partner._ Open communication between dating partners regarding their sexual ideals and values is an excellent way of preventing arousing situations. The key here is to be up front. Let the other person know your limits and values. It isn't fair to invite someone to the airport without saying whether it's for a plane ride or a parachute jump.

This doesn't mean that you introduce yourself by saying, "Hello, I'm Jack and I don't sleep with anyone." You can be both forthright and tactful in letting the other person know your limits. Those who are candid with their dating partner usually receive a positive response.

An easy way of bringing up the subject might be to talk about something from the newspaper as an opener. "This report says more singles today remain celibate prior to marriage than ever before." Or talk about your personal values: "It is only fair to tell you about the values I have chosen for my life. I want to develop dating relationships that do not include sex until marriage. I hope you will respect these values and join me in keeping them."

To be so up front about your no-sex policy with someone you do not yet know well, someone who may not even have approached you sexually, may be a bit stressful. But once out in the open, you will notice it eliminates stress and uncertainty from the relationship.

4. *Develop and abide by a dating agreement.* Face it. Dating as an adult is vastly different from dating as a teenager. When teenagers date, there is less necessity of talking through the goals of their relationship. It's more a trial-and-error period where one person is as interesting as the next. Little by little this adolescent phase passes until maturity is reached and the young adult begins looking for the one person who is right for her.

Most single adults are looking for a life partner. Therefore they must be more discriminating about their dating choices than they were as teenagers. They must talk honestly about the goals of their relationship. After discussing their goals, they can evaluate their compatibility and discuss how much physical contact is desired and how it will serve the goals they've developed.

Dr. Jim Talley, author of *Too Close Too Soon,* recognizes that the rush to sexual intimacy must be brought under control early.[1] According to Dr. Talley's theory, the average couple lands in bed after spending three hundred hours alone together. He encourages the couples he counsels to stretch that time out by having them agree to limit their time together. He recommends no more than twenty hours the first month, thirty hours the second month, forty hours the third month, and fifty hours the fourth month. Time the couple spend alone is counted hour for hour; group time is divided by four; phone time is counted when conversations run over half an hour. Time together must be recorded on a chart.[2]

After the couple has developed a strong and consistent friendship and desires to hold each other physically, the couple enters into "relationship instruction," which extends over a four-month period. After meeting with an instructor, both persons complete homework in workbooks. Many in Dr. Talley's courses are previously married persons who simply do not want to make another mistake and are taking a serious look at building a relationship that will last a lifetime. As we have seen, the previously married often skip the preliminary stages of emotional development in a relationship, allowing the sexual side to dictate and control them.

In addition to this type of exploration of the relationship, the couple sign a commitment to limit their physical involvement as well as their time together. The limits are stringent, and the couple must agree to keep strict limits on both.

Dr. Talley makes a valid point when he emphasizes the value of signing a commitment to celibacy. One man said, "By signing my name and making a commitment, I stopped sleeping around. It was the first step back toward reconciliation with my ex-wife." Anyone who is serious about remaining abstinent until marriage can greatly benefit from such an agreement. Here are some things to consider as you develop your own agreement.

Writing a Dating Agreement
- Discuss with your partner and agree on what level of dating you are presently at, based on the seven stages of dating listed in chapter 3.
- Based on your stage of dating, discuss and state how often you should see each other each week, taking into

account work, family, church, distance, and other responsibilities.

- Discuss the best times to be together, keeping in mind that not much good goes on after 11:00 P.M.

- Discuss and limit the amount of time you will spend alone together.

- Discuss and list activities that you can do together that will assist you in limiting time spent alone together and yet will enhance the development of the emotional, social, and spiritual dimensions of the relationship.

- Discuss and identify places that will be off-limits. This includes places of amusement as well as places where the two of you will be alone, such as bedrooms, motels, and apartments.

- Discuss and agree on the level of pair bonding at which you wish to limit your show of affection for each other (see chapter 10).

- Agree on a plan of action should you even one time go beyond the limits previously set, realizing that at that point you are powerless to control your own behavior. If you encounter trouble in this area, you must enlist a third party who can hold you accountable. If the relationship is valuable to you, the physical side must be brought under control.

- On a monthly basis go over your dating agreement to make sure you are holding to the time and intimacy limits you've set.

5. Develop an action plan should you ever be faced with a "close encounter." You've thought through your values and developed your standards. You will try to live by those standards, but at some point you will be with someone who will tempt you to go beyond those limits, trying to push you over the line. What will you say? What will you do? You

216

must act fast. Advance planning now could save you heartache later on.

Let's look at a threat to your standards in three stages:

A *light threat:* Say no and mean it. Begin telling a long, involved dramatic story. Talk about Christ. Get up, change the activity, and say: "I'm starved. Let's go get something to eat." Tell a joke: "Do you know why the children of Israel wandered in the wilderness for forty years? Even then men wouldn't stop and ask for directions." When there is no serious threat to your standards, any one of these ideas may take care of the situation.

A *medium threat:* This situation is a little more serious. A simple no thank you has not worked. Another tactic must be employed. You may need to use a firmer no through an I-statement: "I feel very threatened when you pressure me in this manner because you show no respect for my wishes." You may need to repeat such a statement twice firmly before the other person comprehends what you are saying. You may need to leave so you are with other people. Women especially need to always carry change for a phone call and twenty dollars for a taxi.

A *serious threat:* Your wishes, standards, and previous deterrents have been disregarded. This is not the time to fear offending the other person's feelings. Trust your instincts— if you feel seriously threatened or scared, act on your feelings. Escape any way you can. Use whatever resources necessary to get away. Slap and run. You may want to carry pepper spray, just in case.

Don't wait for a real threat to occur; develop a plan of action before it happens. Think of it as a practice fire drill. The time to find the exit is before the flames are singeing your feet.

217

6. *Become accountable to someone.* An accountability partner is someone to whom you will be responsible for your conduct. A trusted friend, pastor, counselor, or teacher is a good choice. It could be a group of people to whom you make yourself accountable. Both parties should be comfortable with and respect the person chosen.

An Air Force pilot reentered civilian life totally messed up. In the military he had learned to drink and womanize. After his discharge he continued the same lifestyle in spite of vows to clean up his act. Repeatedly he tried to change on his own. Nothing happened until he joined a support group at his church. He became accountable to the group for a change in lifestyle and he experienced a dramatic difference. Support groups are frequently conducted through churches. Some twelve-step programs have accountability checks that deal severely with members who admit to falling into unacceptable patterns of behavior. But they also offer tremendous strength and support to their members.

A couple who desire to be held accountable for maintaining the standards they have set must report in person weekly to their accountability partner. While looking him or her in the eyes, the couple must give a full account of time, activities, and conduct. Powerful! I recommend it!

7. *Plan your dates carefully in advance.* Before going on a date, know where you are going, who is going to be present, what activities there are to participate in, how you are getting there, and what time you will return home. If a date can't provide this information or hesitates when asked—beware!

Dating should include a variety of interesting activities. Time spent participating in activity dates should far outweigh time spent in spectator dates (see chapter 4). Plan a variety of fun activities, then you will get to know your date's likes and dislikes, total personality, values, goals, and beliefs.

In the early stages of a relationship, group dates are best. The two of you will be together but when you are with friends or another couple there is less stress. This allows you to observe how your date interacts with others and her sense of humor. In a group you can size up your date faster than you ever could on ten formal dates alone. Among friends, he will relax and be himself. It cuts out "masking." Group dating leaves room for friendship to grow.

Group dates also make it easier to maintain moral standards and prevent many dangerous "close encounters." You will not get into "touchy situations" that are not suitable viewing for others.

8. *Choose your dates with care.* You should date people who have similar interests, ideals, and values and who are about your age. Your best dates should come from the circle of friends you have already established, people you know something about. Avoid a blind date with someone you do not know or have never met unless it is arranged by a trusted friend.

Never date married persons, those whose divorce is pending (they are still married), anyone who is drinking or drunk, drug users, and anyone not in a position to date you openly. Don't be so hard up that you would date twice someone who doesn't measure up to your standards.

9. *Avoid situations designed to stimulate sexual pleasure.* I am constantly amazed at those who take daring, calculated risks with their sexual behavior. Couples who spend hours at the beach on a blanket nestled together, necking and fondling by the hour; couples who sleep together without having sex, who lie down and just hold each other, who fondle each other to orgasm without going further are all taking great risks. No one can continue to take such risks and beat all the odds.

Adult singles who live in apartments or own their own homes must lay down strict guidelines regarding their deportment when entertaining opposite-sex partners in their home. Periods of cuddling and cooing in front of a cozy fire can eventually lead to sexual intimacy as can candlelight dinners for two with romantic music and nothing else to do. Not only should you avoid settings that are sexually tempting but also avoid movies, TV, and videos that would encourage sinful desires and fantasies.

One previously married woman made friends with a man in a city a two-hour drive from her home. They alternated visits to each other's city. After several such visits he invited her to dinner at his apartment where he would cook the meal. The meal was enjoyed by candlelight and relished by both. After they watched a video, it was late and she faced the two-hour drive home. He offered her his bedroom while he slept on the sofa. The first time this arrangement worked. The second time it didn't.

Others think they can travel together and share a motel room or go camping and share a tent. Such game playing is foolish. No one can play with sexual fire for long without getting burned. God would have us flee the "appearance of evil" (1 Thess. 5:22 KJV). We are not to flirt with temptation.

Once your limits are defined, stick to your guns. Regardless of how magic the moment, the mood, and the music, remind yourself of your dating agreement and that renegotiation is permitted only in broad daylight, when the passion has cooled, your accountability partner is present, and you have both the time and rationale to rethink your position.

Not only will this help you translate close encounters into rational behavior, but it also allows you to keep intact a very precious commodity—your self-esteem.

10. *Learn to control your sexual desires.* You do not need to give in to your sexual urges just because you have them. The sex drive in both males and females can be denied expression for months, years, or even permanently with no adverse effects. Many men and women never marry or have intercourse and lead normal, happy, productive lives.

This is called sublimation. It means that a person diverts her drives to acceptable outlets. Rather than indulging sexual urges, you look for another form of expression. Many people pursue occupations that absorb their interests and much of their time. Others become involved in active sports, community service, hobbies, service clubs, or church work. To sublimate sexual energy means that you discover and develop interesting activities that provide enough personal satisfaction so that sexual energies can be redirected, not denied.

Sublimation is more beneficial than repression. Repression of your sexual desires means you ignore them, pretend they are not there. Repression only delays the time when an issue must be faced. In sublimation you recognize your drive and deal with it constructively. Sublimation of your sex drive does not mean rejection or denial, but rather that you accept it and take charge of your sexual urges.

Even married persons must learn to control their sexual desires. A physician may recommend that a pregnant woman avoid intercourse for several weeks prior to the birth of a baby and for several weeks following delivery. One of the married partners may take a trip for business or personal reasons that separates one from the other for a period of time. Self-control must be exercised during such times.

Sex desires are very real but they are more real when you are doing nothing. So take your mind off the subject and plunge into an absorbing activity. It is nearly impossible to concentrate on sex if absorbed in directing a choir, helping a youth group perfect their parts in an upcoming drama, or writing an article for a magazine.

Ask God for Help

An important part of your commitment to abstinence is relying on God. Ask your heavenly Father for His help to remain pure. If you and your date discuss and pray about your commitment to abstinence, it will produce a bond of conscience between you that can serve as a barrier against temptation. Discuss your relationship in terms of "we three—God, you, and I."

Sexual immorality is a seductive sin. Two of the most difficult sins to resist are pride and sexual immorality since both are seductive. Pride says, "I deserve it"; sexual desire says, "I need it." In combination, their appeal is deadly. Solomon says that only by relying on God's strength can we overcome them. Pride appeals to the empty head; sexual enticement to the empty heart. But by looking to God we can fill our heads with wisdom and our hearts with His love. You may not be able to resist sexual temptation, but God can. Turn that part of your life over to Him too.

Whenever you are tempted with a "close encounter" here are some powerful Bible verses to help. You may want to memorize some of them. They will boost and reaffirm your convictions to remain sexually abstinent.

Job 31:1	Romans 6:13–14	Galatians 5:16–21
Psalm 101:2–3	1 Corinthians 6:9–10	Ephesians 5:3–5
Psalm 119:9–11	1 Corinthians 6:18–20	Colossians 3:5–8
Matthew 5:27–29	1 Corinthians 10:13	1 Thessalonians 4:3–8

For Those Who Have Already Gone Too Far

What should you do if you and your partner have already proceeded too far in the pair-bonding steps? First of all, you do not need to feel unclean or subhuman. And you are not obligated to marry just because you have had intercourse. Nor are you obligated to marry because of pregnancy. For a couple to marry just to give a baby a name is one of the least valid reasons for marriage.

If you are already involved in a sexual relationship, the remedy will not be easy, but the following suggestions will help.

Admit the sinfulness of your actions. A woman sobbingly confessed to her minister how she and a male friend had been carrying on a sexual affair. Through her tears she said she never meant to become involved with him. It was all a mistake, an accident. She allowed her loneliness to control her emotions and the inevitable happened. She never meant to let it go this far.

Notice all the self-deceiving rationalization. It was an accident. She never meant to let it go this far. This was no accident. Both parties freely and willfully made a series of decisions that permitted and encouraged intercourse. A private place where they could be alone was sought. They progressed from light body fondling to intense body fondling. This was a decision whether they recognized it or not. Both agreed to proceed. She agreed when she allowed fondling below the waist. He decided when he attempted intercourse.

To call such decisions an accident is self-deceiving rationalization. Both partners refused to draw the line at several stopping points. Personal moral values and spiritual principles were tossed to the winds when emotional and sexual arousal gained the upper hand. This is not an accident but a choice, and the sooner a couple admits they are making deliberate choices, the sooner they will be able to handle the problem and cope with the guilt connected with it.

Ask God for forgiveness. Once you admit personal guilt, you can move to the second step and confess your wrong to your heavenly Father. How blessed to possess faith in a Savior who knows all and yet forgives all. Confession cleanses and purifies the soul, and we serve a God who will totally and completely forgive our sins when we truly repent. If we face our wrongs and are sincerely sorry, God has a wonderful way of using these experiences for our good. He can actually help us, through our mistakes, to become stronger, finer, and more complete persons. Your present attitudes toward the experience can help you grow to be a more loving, understanding, and sympathetic person when sin entraps and enslaves others.

So refuse to whip yourself endlessly with guilt. Forget the tears and sleepless nights. Stop punishing yourself. Stop cutting yourself off from spiritual activities because of your guilt. Ask for divine forgiveness and then accept it.

Even though God can forgive your sins, you still have to live with the consequences of your actions. If you lost your virginity so long ago you can't remember where or when, that fact will always be part of you. If you have had a sexually transmitted disease, become pregnant or caused someone to become pregnant, had an abortion, or put a child up for adoption, the recollection will recur from time to time. There's no way of escaping the dreaded reality of the past. But God has an amazing way of healing memories so they won't haunt or destroy you. When God says that He forgives your sins, He means that He not only forgives them but He forgets them as well.

Scripture tells us that He casts our sins into the depth of the ocean. Did you know that the ocean is so deep in places and the pressure so great that anything that drops to the bottom cannot be brought back to the surface? And that's exactly where God casts our sins, in a place where they can never be found again. In this way He frees us to begin again. Your slate is clean in His sight. Your sins are forgiven. It is as though it never happened.

You no longer need to carry self-reproach or guilt concerning the past, only gratefulness to a heavenly Father who is big enough to forgive even sexual sins. Press forward in happiness, honesty, and earnestness.

Stop seeing each other. This is the hard part. If you are currently involved in a sexual relationship you and your partner must stop seeing each other for at least six months. Vowing to stop having sex but continuing to see each other as before won't work. After a couple has become sexually active, it is next to impossible to be together without indulging in sex. It's similar to being addicted to a hard drug; during a sane moment you pledge you will never touch the stuff again but when the craving hits, you can't control yourself.

After not seeing your partner for six months, you will be able to determine if what you have is real love or infatuation. The only way to find out is to isolate the sexual factor. In any scientific experiment, the variable must be isolated. In this case the variable is sex.

Studies indicate that a good sexual relationship can hold a couple together for three to five years, but no longer if that is all they have going for them. For this reason alone a couple should resist sexual temptation early in their relationship. Sex deceives the emotions. A couple need to be very sure of other factors before clouding and complicating the picture with the powerful responses that surface when sex takes over. A couple attempting to sidestep this issue only deceive themselves.

Only the two of you can make the decision to stay apart. An accountability partner can help by providing motivation and encouragement to abide by your decision. Undeniably, this will be a very difficult period for a couple who are really in love but it offers the only way for both of you to analyze the quality of the relationship.

Should your partner be unwilling to forgo sex for this period of time, several things become crystal clear. If your partner is more

> *We can learn something about devotion from cranes, those large, graceful birds with long necks.*
>
> *George Archibald, a scientist in Wisconsin, tells us about a sandhill crane that would come to the same road every night. Archibald learned from a state trooper that the crane's mate had been killed by a car at that spot. The crane would return every night and stare into the distance, waiting for her mate to come back.*
>
> The Dance of Life

interested in filling urgent sexual needs now than in establishing a long-term, emotionally healthy relationship, maybe sex is the only thing you've got going. Before proceeding, find out for sure. Test that relationship for six months! If your partner can't hold out, you know what he was interested in.

Double Protection

You've read to this point but you're not buying it. You remain unconvinced that engaging in sex prior to marriage is wrong for you. You plan to make no changes in your present sexual attitudes or behaviors and will take advantage of the next opportunity that presents itself.

If this is your decision in spite of the evidence, I ask one thing—proceed in the best way possible. This means never having unprotected sex—sex without the use of condoms to protect against sexually transmitted diseases. Although not adequate, the protection condoms provide is a few degrees better than no protection at all. And as long as the possibility of pregnancy exists, protect yourself against pregnancy. Mature women must not be fooled by the early onset of menopause. You can still get pregnant and you need protection. This means *he* uses protection and so does *she*. Unmarried sex calls for double protection!

When taking time to double protect, you may find passionate desires cool slightly and become easier to control. Taking time for protection provides time to think. It isn't very romantic. It's serious and businesslike, but then so are parenthood . . . sexually transmitted diseases . . . abortion . . . pregnancy.

A Choice to Be Proud Of

John Tesh, former cohost of television's *Entertainment Tonight*, and actress Connie Sellecca have learned that good things come to those who wait. This couple, who chose to wait until marriage for sex, have stated that they wanted to do everything right this time.[3] Both were gun-shy about entering a new commitment because each had had a disastrous earlier marriage. After John's first marriage was dragged through the divorce court with the kind of testimony the supermarket tabloids pounce on, John said that every couple should be forced to spend just one day in divorce court before they're given a marriage license. He spent a lot of time in therapy making sure his relationship with Connie was not on the rebound.

After a year's courtship, the couple flew to Carmel, on the coast of California, where they helped serve Thanksgiving dinner in a mission for the homeless. They went on to nearby Monterey for a festive dinner at a restaurant on the water. When they arrived at the restaurant, Connie noticed the empty parking lot and a sign on the door that read "Closed." She hesitated, but John pushed ahead and led her to a table in the center of the deserted restaurant. As she looked around in bewilderment a string quartet began to play "Concetta," a love song John had written for her early in their romance. (Concetta Sellecchia is her real name.)

Suddenly it became clear that John had rented the entire restaurant for the two of them to enjoy. In the middle of their five-course dinner, John dropped to his knees asking for Connie's hand in marriage. How did she respond? Completely overwhelmed, she cried buckets. Her acceptance of his proposal created fireworks. An off-shore barge launched a magnificent ten-minute fireworks display.

But their engagement was not all fireworks, music, and romance. Both Connie and John are deeply committed Christians. They had many serious talks about the responsibilities and demands of sharing their Hollywood lives together and spent thirty hours in premarital counseling with their pastor. In those sessions they learned to handle disagreements. When upset, "I close down," Connie said.

"He likes to talk it through." They read books that probed into marital crises and how to solve them. They role-played. Together they studied the Scriptures. In addition they talked about religion, finances, the importance of communicating on every level, and sex. They jokingly called it a slugfest among four people—Connie, John, the pastor, and God.

But this is the best part. This high-profile couple chose pre-marital abstinence during their courtship—for religious reasons and "to be a good role model to my son," Connie added proudly. That's right. They chose to wait until their wedding night to consummate their vows. Snuggling close to John, Connie said during an interview before their marriage, "Our honeymoon will be traditional in every sense of the word." John added, "This is going to be some honeymoon!"

John Tesh and Connie Sellecca have been good role models not only for her son but for the world. Abstinence is a choice to be proud of.

In the face of temptation, John and Connie were able to overcome because they had learned to deny themselves certain pleasures today in order to attain long-range goals. They knew the beauty of present sacrifice for future rewards.

Most of us think we can choose correctly at the very moment we must make the decision. Instead, we choose according to the way we have chosen a hundred times before. Our future is not what we decide to do, but what we have done in the past. Our future actually lies behind us!

If you want to be a winner, like John and Connie, you too will have to give up some immediate pleasures for the sake of ultimate benefits. You will look away from wickedness rather than accept it as normal. Just as John and Connie chose and followed the law of chastity and purity, so you can live by a code of decency and morality in a world that places little or no value on these attributes. Your future will be determined by your response to choices through obedience to God. The price is high, but the rewards are limitless.

Part 6

Before You
Fall in Love
Again

13

Getting Fit to Be Tied

Cathy Guise from the *Cathy* comic strip says, "I'm beautiful, bright, charming, talented, and ready to share my life with someone, Charlene! I want to dream with someone . . . plan with someone . . . I want to be there for someone, and I want someone to be there for me!"

Charlene responds, "My husband has a really cute friend who . . ."

"Aack!!" Cathy screams. "A fix-up?? Are you out of your mind?? No fix-ups!! I'm ready to be married. I'm not ready to date."

Many singles are like Cathy. Marriage is their goal but they don't want to have to go through the process of preparing successfully to achieve their goal. They desire the prize but aren't willing to pay the price. The price in this case is personal maturity along with insightful preparation and careful evaluation of self, the process, and the other person.

The Scriptures read: "When I was a child, I used to speak as a child, think as a child, reason as a child; when I became a man, I did away with childish things" (1 Cor. 13:11 NASB). When you entered your teens, you put away toys that represented childhood, so when you become mature you put away immaturity.

Getting fit for marriage includes understanding the nature of love and how love develops slowly as you progress through various levels and types of love. Each previous experience with love should have taught you something valuable for the future. By now you recognize that you have loved several persons with whom you could not live. You realize that love must be supported by common interests and goals, acceptance of each other, and mutual respect. You should be able to differentiate between romantic love (infatuation) as pictured in movies and fiction and the type of love that provides lasting happiness in marriage (see chapters 7 and 8).

> *I believe that the sign of maturity is accepting deferred gratification.*
>
> Great Thoughts,
> Funny Sayings

If you are mature, you recognize that marriage is not an easy escape from reality or personal problems, but rather brings on new problems and greater responsibilities. You also understand that marriage offers the most rewards when the relationship is a mutual meeting of personality needs. You recognize that marriage is not just a private matter between two people, but rather it guarantees the stability of the community and protects the security of children. When mature, you recognize these larger implications, as well as the meaning for your personal life.

If you are mature, you have developed a philosophy of life that guides you daily. You have come to terms with your religious concepts, values, and goals and are living in accordance with your beliefs. If you are spiritually mature, you have found your relationship with God to be invaluable, allowing you to cope with problems that surface.

You have evaluated yourself and are aware of your strengths and are working to improve your limitations. Weak areas that are difficult to change, you accept without excessive guilt. You build on strengths and make the most of what you have. You recognize areas of failure but compensate by doing other things well. You have taken a long hard look at your family background, the contribution it has made to making you what and who you are, and what it is from your background that you will bring to marriage. Research shows that the emotional climate of your parents' home greatly influences your chances for success in marriage. If unhappiness has marred your immediate past or if repeated marriage failures have dogged you or generations in your past, you face this realistically and have plotted constructive ways of overcoming obstacles to future happiness. You no longer blame parents for their failures and if you come from a happy family you do not take happiness for granted. Instead, you work hard at understanding the components of successful family living.

Maturity means learning how to meet problems constructively. The frustrations of life do not throw you into fits of confusion, discouragement, or disorganization. You have learned from past experiences and use them as a means of growth in your ability to cope with emergencies and crises. This increases your ability to build a successful marriage.

Maturity means learning about interpersonal relationships. You recognize that inner motivations prompt behavior. You see that aggressive and domineering behavior is often a cover-up for insecurity and that clinging dependence is usually a means of escaping from life's problems. You recognize jealousy as an expression of insecurity or inadequacy and criticism as an attempt to tear down others and build up self. An understanding of what influences behavior helps in evaluating a marriage partner.

Maturity means you can put the wants and needs of your partner before your own—at least part of the time. A *Peanuts* cartoon shows Charlie Brown talking with Lucy. Charlie says, "I'd like to be able to feel that I'm needed."

Lucy responds, "Don't forget, Charlie Brown, that people who are really needed are asked to do a lot of different things."

He thinks it over and responds, "I'd like to feel needed and yet not have to do anything."

How often this kind of love and caring lures us! But it is totally unrealistic. The inability of partners to put themselves out for the other person, to think first of the needs of their partner, accounts for much marital agony.

Maturity means being able to assess your own level of maturity. An immature person will be almost totally unaware of how much growth or change is necessary. The less mature you are, the more quickly you will want to plunge into marriage.

Evaluating Maturity

No one can precisely rate another person's level of maturity, but it is fairly easy to identify signs of dysfunction. Persons exhibiting the following characteristics are marginal in their marriageability quotient. In addition, you should entirely avoid marrying a person with a major dysfunction. It is always risky to classify individuals because of the difficulty in sizing people up and putting them into slots. However, an understanding of how dysfunctional persons act and the extremes that characterize their behavior will indicate that any person who approaches these extremes will make a difficult, if not impossible, mate. The following list of social characteristics betray a dysfunctional individual. Check any that apply to your partner.

Symptoms of a Dysfunctional Person

———— 1. Shows fear and anxiety when faced with new social situations that hold no real threat

———— 2. Expresses guilt that has little or no basis

——— 3. Frequently exhibits intense emotion and excitement inappropriate to the situation: hysterical laughter or tears

——— 4. Displays phobias; shows fear or unwarranted distrust toward certain objects, situations, or ideas that people do not ordinarily fear or distrust

——— 5. Is ritual-ridden; life is unnaturally patterned around the exacting performance of specific tasks in a specific way

——— 6. Has uncontrollable impulses—sudden desires to do particular things regardless of consequences

——— 7. Is obsessed with health—a hypochondriacal concern about personal health, with limitless complaints and pain in various parts of the body

——— 8. Has deep moods of depression, often accompanied by unwarranted guilt feelings

Anyone evidencing one or more of the above symptoms is marginal in his marriageability.

Symptoms of a Seriously Dysfunctional Person

——— 1. Shows extreme shyness, submissiveness, and inability to relax in the presence of others

——— 2. Shows hostility and antagonism toward others, society, government, authority, and the world in general

——— 3. Expresses suspicion and extreme skepticism concerning new people, ideas, and values

——— 4. Makes a conspicuous display of clothing, possessions, and finances in order to impress others—even strangers

——— 5. Shows arrogance and an attitude of condescension around even longtime friends

235

————— 6. Is given to boisterous behavior regardless of where she is

————— 7. Is preoccupied with sex or sex-linked subjects or shows a strong aversion to sex

————— 8. Has an insatiable yearning for excitement and adventure and cannot enjoy quiet times or more subtle forms of pleasure

————— 9. Makes tactless and embarrassing public displays of affection for friends of either sex

————— 10. Is given to lying or distorting facts to put herself in a favorable light

————— 11. Shows an overeagerness to please everyone, even strangers, by doing their bidding, agreeing with their opinions, et cetera

————— 12. Shows extreme dependence and desires to have everything settled and unchanging

Anyone with these symptoms should never be considered as marriageable.

Danger signals connected to emotional instability do not always show up early in a relationship. This is another reason for long courtships prior to marriage. Those who rush toward marriage without recognizing the danger signals often are the least prepared for marriage. If you are in a relationship where a partner exhibits one or more of the symptoms listed above, slow down and begin immediately to investigate underlying problems. Anyone exhibiting these behaviors will make a difficult if not impossible mate.

Don't ignore danger signals, especially when you are desperately in love or think your partner might be able to solve your problems. Don't waste time after finding out she is crazy, on drugs, married, or a total flake. Look for warning signs early in a relationship. That's why I advise a long period of friendship first. During this period of unemotional involvement, many of these problems will become evident.

You aren't helpless and you don't need to plunge into a relationship blind. Take control. If you want to find out something about your partner, ask. If she isn't talking or says she has no family or friends anywhere, that's a real red flag. Plan a social get-together with your friends and your intended's friends. Ask probing questions and listen carefully to what is said about the person. You'll likely hear many clues that may or may not signal problems.

Take off your rose-colored glasses and begin to do some serious investigation. You deserve to know the facts. A person with something to hide will rarely admit it. The usual defense is to blow up and try to make you feel guilty for asking. She may accuse you of not trusting her or acting like a mother.

If friends and others speak well of the person and she has demonstrated honesty and integrity in everything that is said and done, you will likely be able to trust the information you've been given.

Some people marry quickly to avoid facing danger signals. A compulsive mechanism drives them to the altar regardless of evident obstacles. Personality testing along with a counselor's advice is helpful. But there is still no substitute for a long period of courtship. Only after a long friendship will masks slip and the real self emerge.

Live-in Lovers

You've been dating someone terrific. She's considerate, fun, and a great conversationalist. You think you have found the real thing. Obviously she feels the same about you because after a delightful afternoon at the lake, she pops the question. "We have something special here. How about moving in with me?" Before you pack, look at the cold, hard facts.

Living together before marriage is an almost sure predictor of failure. According to psychologist David G. Myers, Ph.D., author of _The Pursuit of Happiness,_ seven recent studies concur that couples who live together before marriage have a higher divorce rate than those who don't. Three

237

studies in the United States show that a couple who live together before marriage are more likely to separate or divorce within ten years. A national Canadian survey of 5,300 women found that those who lived together were 54 percent more likely to divorce within fifteen years. And a Swedish study of 4,300 women found cohabitation linked with an 80 percent greater risk of divorce.[1]

Their divorce rate is higher because the couple are less committed to the relationship and thus more likely to divorce. Their skepticism about the durability of the relationship prevents them from giving their marriage the gung-ho push needed to succeed.

A comprehensive survey done by the National Survey of Families and Households, based on thirteen thousand interviews, concluded, "About 40 percent of cohabiting unions in the U.S. break up without the couple getting married. . . . And marriages that are preceded by living together have 50 percent higher disruption (divorce or separation) rates than marriages without premarital cohabitation"! That makes for a 75 percent divorce rate rather than 50 percent. Another way to state those statistics might be: Of every one hundred couples who begin living together, forty will break up before marriage. Of the sixty who marry, forty-five will divorce. That leaves only fifteen of the original couples still married. Society tells us to try the shoe on before buying it, but this is not true when applied to marriage. The odds are four to one against a live-in relationship developing into a lasting marriage.

More than half of all recent marriages have been preceded by the couple living together. The number is even higher when a remarriage is involved—when one or both have been divorced. Two-thirds of recent remarriages are preceded by cohabitation.

What's behind this trend? A desire by the couple to "try out" their compatibility before making a commitment. Many adult children of divorce want to live with a partner

238

first to avoid the mistakes of their parents. One study revealed that 51 percent of the males and 56 percent of the female cohabitors believed that living together before marriage would prove compatibility.[2]

Many people are aware of such statistics but discount the data as they feel their situation is different. But as Dr. Laura Schlessinger puts it in _Ten Stupid Things Women Do to Mess Up Their Lives,_ "Why are you willing, even eager, to play Russian roulette with your life? Why? Desperation. Fear of not having somebody—of not having a life if a man doesn't want you."[3]

Moving in with someone prior to marriage is an act of immaturity. There is no commitment. It blasts a loud message: "You don't have to do much to get me." Then your live-in buddy fools around. You stay, and another deafening message comes through: "You don't have to do much to keep me either." Furthermore, according to the _Journal of Marriage and the Family,_ "aggression is at least twice as common among cohabitors as it is among married partners." In addition, "cohabitors also experience significantly more difficulty in [subsequent] marriages with [issues] of adultery, alcohol, drugs and independence than couples who had not cohabited."[4] All of these messages are devastating blows to self-esteem.

Living together is a difficult trap to break out of. When you are dating, if someone is immature or disrespectful or abuses you verbally or physically, you can back off and not date the person again. But once you're living together, it becomes more difficult to end what needs to be ended. You keep hoping and praying your partner will change. And after a year of living together, separating can be as painful as divorce—especially for women.

Live-together couples who eventually do marry are less happy in marriage. Women are especially unhappy with the quality of communication after the wedding. While living together, each may be afraid to complain about irritating habits, express anger, or state how he or she really feels. After all, one gripe too many might send the other packing. This sets up a faulty communication system and leaves the couple powerless to commit after saying, "I do."

When asked why they are living with a partner, the number one reason cited by women is that they want to get married. Yet few live-in relationships result in marriage. One study concluded that only one in three cohabiting couples tie the knot. And a Columbia University study showed only 26 percent of the women surveyed and a scant 19 percent of the men married the person they were living with.[5]

Cohabiting males give a totally different reason for living with a partner before marriage. The number one reason cited by males is sex. As one male put it, "Living together provides safe sex, when you want it, how you want it." One study found that 40 percent of cohabiting women had endured a kind of sex they didn't want or enjoy and that live-in lovers are less considerate than husbands. Studies also conclude that live-in arrangements favor men, not women.[6]

Marriage has some definite advantages. It acts as a safeguard for moral standards, property rights, and joint purchases. It also provides a legitimate name for children. Marriage laws prevent bigamy, fraud, the use of force, and the marriage of children or of a seriously incompetent person. It guards the legality of the wedding agreement and comes with many built-in protections. *Living together offers no legal protection.*

Marriage offers a couple the opportunity for happiness, though it does not provide them with the wherewithal to achieve it. There is no magic in the wedding itself to change persons or circumstances. There is no love potion that guarantees a couple will live "happily ever after." No words spoken on the wedding day teach a couple how to achieve lasting bliss. Whatever happiness is achieved results from personal effort, knowledge, love, and commitment. The wedding itself makes few internal changes, but it does make dramatic changes in status, rights, and opportunities. Live-in lovers might find it possible to avoid divorce lawyers and alimony, but often there are no fewer problems, heartaches, or tears.

The Most Important Factors When Selecting a Mate

A well-adjusted and mature person can marry any one of several persons and be happy. An immature person will never be happily married to anyone. Marriage does not make an immature person mature, but happy and mature people do make successful marriages.

Although the number of persons you could successfully mate with is large, this does not mean that you could make a go of marriage with just anyone. You must still choose wisely. What, then, should you look for in an ideal mate? There are ten characteristics that more than anything else determine a person's marriage-ability. They are:

> *Second marriage:*
> *Another instance of the triumph of hope over experience.*
>
> Great Thoughts,
> Funny Sayings

1. superior happiness of parents
2. childhood happiness
3. lack of conflict with mother
4. home discipline that was firm but not harsh
5. strong attachment to mother
6. strong attachment to father
7. lack of conflict with father
8. parental frankness in sex education
9. infrequency and mildness of childhood punishment
10. attitude toward sex that is free from disgust or aversion

Interpersonal relationships during the early years, the example parents have provided, and the attitudes and training they have passed to their children are the most important factors in preparation for marriage. Many studies point to their importance and they should not be overlooked when selecting a mate.

Happiness runs in families—and so do divorce and unhappiness. Early years with parents predispose persons toward success or failure in life. Patterns learned early in life are frequently carried into marriage and acted out then.

No one is bound by his background, however. Just as no one is guaranteed a happy marriage just because his parents were happy, no one is doomed to failure because of unhappy parents. What is necessary, though, is that regardless of background, marriage be approached intelligently through premarital guidance—especially if you have been married before.

A Serious Look at Divorce Insurance

You can tell they are in love. Their eyes light up and their hearts are doing back flips. Eyes and hands are locked. They think they are meant for each other—but this couple is going to make sure. Instead of spending time dreaming, preparing the guest list, browsing through bridal magazines, and discussing food for the reception, they are making notes in a workbook. Laughter breaks the silence. Discussion follows. How much time should we spend separately? With friends? Who will write the checks? Balance the checkbook? Pay taxes? Decide what TV programs to watch? What birth control methods to use? Where to go for holidays? Hmmmmmm. There's no laughter now as they get serious.

Sound unromantic? Unappealing? Maybe. But this is precisely what couples need to do to insure happiness and prevent divorce. Many pastors are requiring couples who want to marry to submit to a rigorous premarital guidance program. Before they can wed, these couples attend weekend seminars, study scriptural wisdom, receive premarital counseling, read books, complete workbook activities clarifying expectations for their relationship, and agree to limit their time together.

A Gallup study showed that more than one third (38 percent) of people who have divorced report they were aware of the problem at the time of marriage or soon afterward. This proves the theory that couples tend to ignore relationship problems when dating—drifting around them with rose-colored optimism. When a problem is encountered, the tendency is to minimize its seriousness, thinking it unimportant or that it can be corrected after marriage. As the romance wears off, however, the problems become glaringly more apparent.

The Gallup Poll came to this critical conclusion: "In an era of increasingly fragile marriages, a couple's ability to communicate is the single most important contributor to a stable and satisfying marriage."[7] The most important single goal of any couple approaching marriage then should be to improve their communication skills.

Yet most couples "in love" have the illusion that communication is easy, feel that they are each other's best friend, and say they can talk about anything. Those who are aware of communication problems don't know what to do about them and think their problems can be solved later. The fact is they can't improve their communication skills on their own any more than they could teach themselves to read and write on their own.

Most churches require engaged couples to have only two or three counseling sessions in which most of the discussion focuses on planning the wedding service. If a couple wishes to be married in a month, and the pastor is willing, their wishes are granted. There is no required waiting period, no required reading, no training in communication skills, no compatibility testing. A few general questions may be directed at the couple about some problems they may have. That's it. Larger churches may offer more stringent programs but most small churches offer no structured program. A church that functions in this manner becomes only a "blessing machine" for tomorrow's divorces. A couple who desire to build a marriage that will last a lifetime should find a pastor or counselor who will provide an extensive premarital guidance program.

An effective premarital guidance program should include a required waiting period, compatibility testing, a premarital course, work with a mentor couple, a rigorous self-study program, and counseling with a pastor.

A Required Waiting Period

A waiting period of six to nine months from the time a couple contacts the pastor until the marriage date should be required. Pastors should be teaching congregations that marriage is more than a wedding day and that time is needed to prepare for something as crucial as marriage. A couple contemplating marriage should not be able to book the church or pastor for a date until they have completed a minimum of six months of premarital counseling, testing, and marriage-preparation seminars. Regardless of the arguments given by couples to hurry things up, the church must stand firm and not allow a couple to rush into marriage—for any reason.

Compatibility Testing

An instrument called PREPARE (Premarital Personal and Relationship Evaluation) is a useful tool for predicting a couple's compatibility.[8] The 125 questions zero in on ten crucial areas. The man and woman answer the questions separately. The test takes about thirty minutes and is computer scored. A pastor or counselor can easily interpret this excellent couple profile. PREPARE gives an objective diagnosis of relationship strengths and weaknesses as well as assessing conflict-resolution ability.

The best time for a couple to take PREPARE is when they are beginning to think about marriage or at least six months before the wedding to see if they have dealt with potential problem issues. There is also a version of PREPARE for couples with children from a previous marriage called PREPARE-MC (Married with Children). The issues facing such couples are much more complex and difficult than for other couples. The MC version assists couples in focusing on the impact of children from previous marriages on a new marriage. In the flush of romance this impact is often underestimated. In thirty minutes PREPARE enables couples to identify where they stand on ten important issues in life. This would take weeks or months to do in casual conversation or counseling.

The most remarkable element of PREPARE is that it can predict with astonishing accuracy which couples will divorce! Dr. H. Norman Wright, a well-known Christian author on marriage, says that PREPARE predicts with 86 percent accuracy which couples will divorce and with 78 percent accuracy which couples will stay happily married. Dr. Wright trusts the prediction. A tenth of those who take PRE-PARE decide not to marry. This is a wise decision when the instrument has predicted a high probability of unhappiness.

The Taylor-Johnson Temperament Analysis (TJTA) is another valuable resource.[9] Unlike PREPARE it compares personality types of individuals: nervous versus composed, depressive versus lighthearted, sympathetic versus indifferent, for example. Each person describes himself and his partner. Both then look at each other's descriptions and talk about them.

Such testing should include several follow-up sessions when the person administering the test meets with the couple to go over the results. Special attention should be given to conflict areas revealed through testing.

Premarital Courses

Engaged Encounter is a weekend retreat for engaged couples lasting from Friday evening to Sunday afternoon. It is intensive and effective. The weekend consists of eighteen talks led by trained married couples and pastors. This is followed by sessions when each couple meets privately and writes reflections in response to questions suggested by the lead couple. After reading each other's answers, the couple dialogue about them. The relaxed atmosphere of an entire weekend allows discussion of key issues likely to be encountered during marriage, including conflict resolution, sexual relations, children, finances, friendships, church participation, and marital goals. Nearly a tenth of those who attend Engaged Encounter decide not to marry or to postpone their wedding. Rather than being a sign of failure, this indicates a strong program. With 50 percent of all marriages and 60 percent of second marriages ending in divorce, the engagement process should be rigorous enough to break weak relationships before marriage.

> *It seems, in fact, as though the second half of a man's life is made up of nothing but the habits he has accumulated during the first half.*
>
> Great Thoughts,
> Funny Sayings

I heartily recommend attending as many marriage seminars or dating and courtship seminars as possible. Couples who are serious about their future can greatly benefit by examining their relationship in light of the subject matter and workbook assignments.

Work with a Mentor Couple

Few people are better equipped to help couples begin married life than a mature couple with a solid marriage. Every church has some couples who would gladly assume a mentor role, if asked and if trained. Such people are a great untapped resource for saving marriages. An engaged couple can quickly identify with a married couple who is willing to share how they have solved problems as encountered. Pastors are less able to be candid about problems in their marriage because of the need to maintain the "pastoral image." A mentor couple is more likely to be transparent and consequently more credible. Furthermore, premarital counseling is usually done by the pastor alone, not the pastor and his wife. Mentoring includes both husband and wife who can impart wisdom from both a male and female point of view. A pastor who takes mentoring seriously will train and use mentors, effectively multiplying his ministry manyfold.

A Rigorous Self-Study Program

Couples can be guided through a self-study program by either the pastor or a mentor couple. I have written several books designed for just such a purpose. The workbooks contain guidelines for self-study. These books include _The Compleat Marriage, The Compleat Marriage Workbook, The Compleat Courtship, The Compleat Courtship Workbook,_ and _How to Talk So Your Mate Will Listen and Listen So Your Mate Will Talk._ This last book is my effort to help couples improve critical communication skills. Here the primary need is not the reading but experience-based verbal and written communication exercises that equip a couple to transform their romance into a lifelong, rewarding marriage. The workbooks are designed to spark deep thought and discussion in critical areas of values and belief systems with topics such as in-laws, sex, finances, parental background, and expectations.

Today many people are marrying for the second or more times. Such persons are less likely to seek premarital counseling in subsequent marriages. The older a couple is, the more likely they are to marry with little or no period of engagement or premarital guidance. A workbook has been designed specifically for those who are remarrying by H. Norman Wright titled *Before You Remarry* (Harvest House, 1988). Critical areas are addressed that might be missed in other programs where a previous marriage doesn't exist.

Counseling with the Pastor

All of the previous guidance components are recommended in addition to whatever counseling the pastor feels is appropriate. After all the previous efforts, a couple still need to seriously study Scripture related to marriage. They need to learn what it means to have a Christ-centered marriage and how to attain it. It should not be assumed that because both persons are Christians or church members, they know how to make Christ the head of their home.

14

Second Chances

The Agony and Ecstasy of Remarriage

You clutch your divorce papers in your hand. At last you are free, free, free! Now you can put the past behind you and look to the future. Or can you? The legal work may be over, but the emotional work may be just beginning. Divorce is painfully destructive and, as a cure, worse than the "disease" itself. Excruciating pain usually accompanies the breaking of a relationship as intimate as marriage, and the pain is more intense and complicated when children are involved.

One reason divorce is so devastating is because of the rejection that accompanies it. To the same degree that falling in love is exciting, falling out of love can hurt. The sense of rejection that follows gnaws at self-esteem and may make you question whether you have any sense of self left, if anyone will ever want you again, and if it is possible for you to love once more. You may have initiated the divorce. Perhaps you were not at fault, did not desire the divorce, were the "innocent party." Or you may have tried to keep the marriage intact. Whatever the circumstances you cannot escape the emotional crisis that accompanies divorce.

Most people agree that divorce is more painful than the death of a loved one. In death the relationship is over and done with. Only memories linger on. But in divorce a relationship still exists—especially when children are shared. Many couples have said, "If children are involved, divorce is never over!"

Try as you may, most formerly married persons can't escape their former partners. More than half of all divorced people admit that their ex-partner is the first one they call in cases of emergency. Holidays become the most psychologically torturous times of the year, with Thanksgiving and Christmas bringing on major migraines. Every continuing encounter is a reminder of failure and rejection. The question of whether the ex-partner will return lingers. Former in-laws and friends further complicate the issue. And if a person enjoyed a regular sexual relationship within the bounds of holy matrimony, what is she to do following divorce?

In a study that followed divorcing partners for a five-year period after the divorce, only 25 percent appeared capable of coping adequately with life. Fifty percent muddled along in a "barely coping" capacity. The remaining 25 percent failed to recover or looked back with intense longing to times before the divorce, wishing the divorce had never taken place. Rather than solving problems, sometimes all divorce does is give people an entirely new set of problems.

Someone has said that divorce is emotional surgery given without anesthesia. There are four cycles or stages of divorce:

1. *Denial.* Early in the process there is shock. To protect yourself you put up emotional padding by saying, "In God's eyes, we'll always be married" or "He'll come back; I just know it" or "When he comes back, I'll make him so happy

he'll wish he'd never left." This is denial of the reality of what has happened!

Denial manifests itself in different ways. Some people withdraw. They move, stop going to church, or refuse to see friends. Others throw themselves feverishly into work. Some get involved in superficial relationships.

Denial is also manifested through co-dependence. The story of the divorce and all the particulars must be retold. Five years later, the divorced person is still saying, "poor me," and looking for a rescuer. Others bargain with their former mate, "I'll do anything you want if you'll only come back" or "If you don't come back, I'll kill myself."

Still another symptom of denial is euphoria. Excess energy is poured into everything attempted. The person is too happy, laughing too much, feeling too good, all in an attempt to forget or deny real feelings. "I'm doing well. Life is good. No problems." In time most people move beyond this level, but it is a real problem if a person stays here.

2. *Feelings of worthlessness.* Overwhelming feelings of having no value and being a total failure dominate this cycle. Anyone who has lived through the nightmare of divorce or dealt with anyone going through it knows this cycle well. Many divorced people suffered from low self-esteem prior to the divorce, but now self-worth plunges to a new low. Bruce Fisher found that divorced people have lower self-esteem than any other group tested.[1] The one who leaves the relationship, the "dumper," has usually practiced divorce emotionally for years. When the marriage finally ends, she suffers from guilt, which reinforces low self-worth. The one on the receiving end, the "dumpee," wants to save the marriage and feels rejected, which results in low self-worth.

Jim Smoke in *Growing in Remarriage* says that 75 percent of those in his divorce recovery seminars have been left for someone or something else. The remaining 25 percent left their marriage due to abuse, perversion, drugs, or other difficult situations in which they felt they could not survive.[2] In both cases, a feeling of rejection is the primary result. After massive doses of rejection and a failed marriage, self-esteem hits an all-time low; good judgment is clouded—another reason to avoid romantic involvements for a time. It will take months and possibly years to regain the self-confidence and emotional stability you once had. Until you accomplish this, you will be operating from a point of weakness and vulnerability rather than from strength and self-assurance.

3. *Total emotional turmoil.* This stage is characterized by intense grief and anger. Feelings that have been bottled up and held beneath the surface break through and the person feels totally overwhelmed. She will lash out uncontrollably at those around her and often cry at inappropriate times over insignificant things. This is typical of people who are grieving. Divorced people must grieve the loss of dreams, values, beliefs, and a marriage partner. Often they will also lose children, a home, church, friends, possessions, finances, and the support of people once depended on. The divorced person must face and grieve the loss so that she can let go of a dead relationship.

Such crushing losses may cause intense rage at the other person or the anger may be turned on self, resulting in depression. Overwhelming bitterness and vindictiveness because of the unfairness of it all may consume a person. She may feel that life is totally out of control and there is no power to change anything.

4. *Letting go.* The fourth and final stage is letting go. This is something that cannot be accomplished in a couple of months. It is a complicated stage and involves forgiveness of others as well as forgiveness of self. From this stage a person can emerge whole and free to love again.

Many divorced persons attempt to shut the door on the past rather than take responsibility for their part in it. Undoubtedly this is one reason for the 60 percent failure rate of second marriages, compared to the 50 percent failure rate for first marriages. Those who don't learn from their mistakes are destined to repeat them.

Working through all this takes time. University of Massachusetts research professor Robert S. Weiss, an expert on divorce and other types of loss, says that it takes a minimum of two if not closer to four years to "gain a sense of what happened, neutralize the painful memories, and establish a new way of life."[3] By the letting-go period the toughest part of the divorce journey is over. This is when the divorced person will grow the most and a good foundation can be laid for a new life. Don't rush it! And don't embrace a quick remarriage as an antidote for a broken spirit.

Reentering the Dating Game

Family and friends often encourage a divorced person to get out of the house and date to get her mind off problems. Their thinking is that this will ease the pain. What it really does is retard personal growth. A person simply must find out who she is as a single person before again entering the dating scene. And as we have seen, it will take months for this to happen.

During this time a divorced person must bring closure to the previous marriage. Divorce is more of a process than an event. No doors can be opened and closed overnight, regardless of what the courts or others say. The closure is similar for widows and widowers. The difference is that divorce leaves many bad memories, and death usually leaves only good memories.

Author Jim Smoke has identified three categories that those recovering from divorce fall into (his descriptive titles tell all): "The Forever Bitter and Battered," "The Quickly Rescued and Remarried," and "The Growing and Guarded."[4] The first two are self-destructive. The third group is the only one moving toward health and responsibility.

253

You can recognize recovery, when a person is ready to enter a new relationship emotionally free. That person feels good about life, has adequate energy for daily living, is not assailed by self-accusations and past memories, and is optimistic and hopeful about the future.

In a remarkable study, fifty-five people were interviewed as they were being admitted to a nursing home. They were asked how much freedom they had in coming to the home, how many other options were available to them, and how much coercion relatives used to get them there. Of the seventeen who said their only alternative was the nursing home, sixteen were dead within ten weeks. But among the thirty-eight who chose the nursing home themselves, only one died.[5] With choices comes hope. Hope brings life.

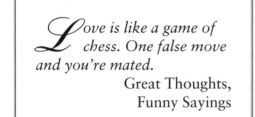

Love is like a game of chess. One false move and you're mated.

Great Thoughts,
Funny Sayings

It should be clear why dating is dangerous during the first three stages of divorce recovery. Attempting to build a relationship when you are in denial, feel totally worthless, or are in emotional turmoil, is futile—at least if you want a healthy relationship.

Dating before your self-worth is intact again can short-circuit your personal growth. When you begin dating, you direct energy toward establishing a new relationship and you decrease automatically the time and energy spent on self-improvement. A new relationship will steal your focus and siphon energy needed for your journey toward wholeness. Spending time with a new person is more exciting and fun than working alone on your self-esteem, but you will pay a heavy price later on because your personal growth will be stunted. To have a happy long-term relationship and certainly before you remarry, the journey toward wholeness must be completed.

A person who is still suffering from a divorce needs twenty-four-hour private-duty care. If that's how you want to spend your time for the next two to four years with no one to care for your own emotional needs, go ahead. But eventually you too will break down.

I'm not advising that divorced persons be shunned. That is not my point. My suggestion is to avoid persons whose divorces are not final and those who have not worked through the denial, problems with self-esteem, and the emotional turmoil. A separated or recently divorced person is often searching for someone to make her pain go away, but no one can make the pain go away. It must be dealt with and that takes time. Healing is often a lonely experience.

As people move through the stages of divorce, progress rarely goes consistently in a positive direction. There is much slipping back and forth among stages until the final stage has been reached. Even then, expect relapses.

It's during this time frame of two to four years following a divorce that you need to be most careful in dating. The tendency is to rush. The exhilaration of finding a new partner brings on surges of romantic affection that can sweep even the most level-headed person off her emotional feet. It is essential now that the relationship be slowed and the fever pitch cooled off. Time is needed for both of you to develop an unhurried relationship where the periods of physical excitement and high-flying emotions do not dominate. No decision about the permanency of a relationship should be made during these two to four years of post-divorce adjustment.

Darrin tells a classic story of what can happen. Darrin was forty-two years old and never married. He was an aggressive, hardworking man caught up in building his business when he finally slowed down enough to realize he wanted a female partner and he began looking. When you live in a small town in upper Minnesota, few choices exist. He dated the women available and after two years emerged shaken and discouraged. One day a business partner asked if Darrin would be interested in dating his sister, Christy, who was coming for a visit.

Darrin was totally unprepared for Christy's physical beauty and her magnetic personality. It was a case of love at first sight. For two weeks the two were hardly ever apart. They went boating, waterskiing, picnicking, and they took long walks in the evening. They talked and talked and talked and talked. Darrin said they talked so much that he felt they packed two years of talking into two weeks. He felt he knew everything there was to know about her and that they had established an intimacy level that others never approach.

Their courtship lasted three months. During that time Darrin learned that Christy had just left an abusive second marriage; her divorce became final during those three months. He learned little about her first marriage except that she had a child and the father had custody.

Three months after meeting, Darrin and Christy were married. Even the honeymoon glow was not allowed to burn itself out on this one. Although he only made mental note of it at the time, on their wedding night he asked how she would feel if she got pregnant so soon after they married. "No problem," she responded glibly. "I'll get an abortion. I've had five others." Things went downhill rapidly from there. More serious problems emerged—among them the fact that she owed the IRS forty-five thousand dollars.

Three months after they were married, Darrin came home one day to find a note saying his bride had gone back to husband number two (the abuser from whom she had barely escaped with her life). Darrin had waited forty-two years to make the right decision but because he got caught in the fever pitch of that early romantic feeling, he got trapped by an emotionally unhealthy person with unfinished business who looked to him to solve her problems. Now his emotional life was in shambles; he was almost unable to go to work and in danger of losing his entire business.

Stay on the safe side. Make no early commitments following divorce or the death of a spouse. There is a dangerous false intimacy that can fool even the most intuitive person. The only safe route at this time is to develop a large circle of friends and stay in groups. Marriage on the rebound rarely works.

Understanding the Loss

To establish a healthy relationship during this period of adjustment, you need to understand your loss. You may wrongly assume that if you could only connect with another person it would take your pain away. This is not the answer. The alienation felt during these stages is due to the multiple losses you have suffered and cannot be replaced by a new love.

Everyone's experience is different, but losses in general might be summed up as follows: You have lost what is known and familiar. You may not have been happy in your marriage but at least you knew what to expect. Now you are adrift on a sea of uncertainty.

There is a loss of valued relationships, activities, and surroundings. People who were friends of you and your spouse may now avoid both of you. You don't attend functions as a family anymore. You may have lost your home and familiar possessions. Nothing is the same as it used to be.

There is also a loss of confidence in your ability to meet life's demands as well as to meet people in the business and social world. Your identity is in crisis. You used to be a family person, with a mate and children. Who are you now? Social identity has to do with whom we are connected or not connected to and what we do with whom. The loss of a partner drastically affects our identity. Acceptance of a new identity as a successful single takes time.

It is very important to have friends during this time but not intimate relationships. Multiple, rather than exclusive

257

friendships, provide contact with others and help you learn who you are as a single adult.

Dating during Divorce

Everyone who has been through the throes of divorce has faced the pressure from others to date during this period. Four very valid reasons exist for not dating until the divorce is final.

First, until the divorce is final you are still married.

Second, there is always a chance for reconciliation until the final decree is signed. Andre and Toni had been separated for months awaiting their final decree. Toni had someone lined up to marry. Andre had met someone he was interested in but would not pursue the relationship until the divorce was final. Just before the divorce was to be final, Toni shocked her attorney by announcing that she wanted to try again with Andre. Toni and Andre are reunited and striving toward a full reconciliation. What would have happened if Andre had thrown in the towel and begun dating someone else?

Third, the recently divorced person is not emotionally ready to date. One couple began dating while each of them was separated from their mate. Each felt God had placed the other there to help them through their loneliness and depression. As soon as their respective divorces were final, they married. Now they realize it was little more than mutual commiseration. The sharing of loneliness and hurt held them together, not a clear-minded decision or even love. This could only be seen after time had passed. Now they face another divorce on the heels of the first one.

Fourth, it isn't fair to the one dating the almost-divorced person. Valerie and Carl met shortly after Carl and his wife separated. Their friendship blossomed within several months to a devoted relationship. Carl's court date was postponed due to custody and property hassles. Without warning, Carl's wife wanted to reconcile. Carl now had a difficult dilemma on his hands. Although he truly sought God's will and knew reconciliation would be advisable and preferable for all involved, he was in love with Valerie. Carl was forced to put his feelings for Valerie on hold and he had to ask Valerie to put her feelings for him on hold. After several attempts, Carl and his wife reconciled. Although Valerie voluntarily chose to enter the relationship with a married man, she went through tremendous pain. Christians, especially, must take seriously their responsibility not to hurt others by choice.

Next to my two-year rule, the strongest advice I give to singles is not to begin dating too soon after a divorce and certainly not before the divorce is final.

Playing the Game Honorably

As single-again adults reenter the dating game, they tend to make up their own rules, feeling there are no clear-cut guidelines for adults and anything goes. A strong Bible-based moral standard is needed. Dating is a much more serious undertaking for mature adults than for teenagers for whom every person they date is not a potential life partner. Mature adults must play the game honorably.

Playing the game honorably means that following a date, especially if it is late at night, you will not enter each other's home. It means you will not take vacations together and share sleeping accommodations, stay overnight in one another's home, and spare me the details of relationships where you are sleeping together but not having sex! It is more honorable for a man to say goodnight at the door.

Playing the game honorably also means that most of the time you will date in groups, particularly in the early stages of dating. Picnics, concerts, and sporting activities with friends are relaxed settings and excellent times for you to get to know another person.

It is often difficult for adult singles, who have had prior experience and possibly a prior marriage, to restrict physical liberties. Playing the game honorably means developing and abiding by a strict moral code. Even though the expression of physical affection may be very natural to you, you will restrict physical intimacy to avoid a broken heart and ruined reputations for both of you.

Dating and the Single Parent

When a parent dates, the child's reaction is unpredictable. Some children are relieved and welcome the fact that Mom or Dad has a love interest. Others resent losing a parent's attention. Some children are rude to a parent's date. One child said to his mother's date while she was out of the room, "Why don't you leave? We don't need you around here."

Some children are more passive and internalize what they think about their parent's date life. They may sulk, pout, and develop behavior problems. Open communication with a child is needed during this time. But let your child remain a child and not a confidante regarding your love life. Be sensitive to the feelings of teenagers who may feel threatened with two generations of daters under one roof. The teenager may feel that it's the privilege of kids, not parents, to date. It may seem like competition when two generations, parent and teen, dress up and present themselves appealingly to the opposite sex.

Some children attempt to matchmake. This can become embarrassing, especially if they ask if a date is going to become their next mommy or daddy. This is an attempt on the child's part to meet her needs and should not be punished or ridiculed. The parent should talk to the child about her feelings, helping the child feel loved and secure.

When Children Don't Approve

When a child's attitude toward a dating partner is negative, you'll need to slow down and think through the consequences. If you disregard your child's feelings she may think you are siding with a stranger against the child. Respectfully listen and regard the child's feelings, letting her know that you will take the feelings expressed into consideration. Also convey in a most considerate and respectful manner that in the end you will make your own decision based on your best judgment. By all means avoid a rebellious attitude, implying that you will do what you want regardless of what the child wants. In a very few years this same child will be choosing a mate. You won't want this attitude coming back to haunt you.

Informing Children

Many question how involved children should be in the dating lives of their parents. The consensus among the experts seems to be that dating lives and children should be kept separate. I tend to agree, at least until a couple is at stage 5 (pre-engagement) or 6 (formal engagement) of dating and is trying to integrate as a family. Children need permanence in their lives. They have already suffered through the dissolution of their family. It's too much to ask of a child to be emotionally involved in a succession of relationships that you may have. To protect younger children from temporary relationships, the wise parent will in most cases keep his dating and family life separate.

You can, of course, occasionally include your friend in some family outings, but only as a "friend" and only on occasion until you are certain he will be a permanent part of your life. Otherwise many problems arise. Should the relationship break up, the children who may have grown to love this person will lose a friend and will suffer from the breakup as well. Keeping distance between your children and your date prevents a date from using the children as pawns to get to the heart of Mom or Dad.

Displays of affection should always be kept private, especially if there is a child. The subject of marriage should not be discussed with a child prematurely and only after it has been a matter of serious discussion between you and your prospective partner. When you do talk with the children, have a private talk without your prospective mate present. Tell your children that you are thinking about marrying this person. Ask them how they feel about it but make it clear that you are not asking their permission. Consider carefully all they have to say and then tell them that you will prayerfully make a decision.

Marrying a Divorced Person

A never-married woman in her early forties visited her minister for what she considered routine premarital counseling. She chatted happily about her wedding plans and asked for any advice he might give her. She also requested that he not reveal her plans to her mother, whom she had not told of the engagement because she didn't know how to break the news that her fiancé had only recently been divorced. No one in the family had ever been divorced, and she felt her mother might be prejudiced concerning her marriage to a divorced person. "His past has no bearing on our future together. That is over and done with. It was not his fault. Divorce is so common now and it would be silly to reject him just because he has been married before!"

Marriage to a divorced person is not the same as when both partners are marrying for the first time. Certainly no one need feel like a second-class citizen because of a divorce. Nonetheless, a divorce does change things. A second marriage is far more complicated than a first marriage. Let's take a look at some of the complicating factors.

Society looks differently at second marriages than first marriages. Society and traditional religious groups smile with approval on first marriages. The marriage is actively supported and celebrated with enthusiasm and anticipation of a happy life for the bridal couple. For a second marriage there is often less enthusiasm. There is often disapproval, although it may not be obvious. Many friends and relatives of the couple assume a wait-and-see attitude. They don't manifest the optimistic acceptance that usually accompanies first marriages. The bridal shower, given by friends, may be symbolic of the attitude. If neither the bride nor the groom has been married before, friends almost always give a shower. If both have been married before, only about one-third receive showers. Family, friends, and society come to the aid of first marriages more often than they do second marriages.

Family opposition. There is a strong likelihood of family opposition to a marriage when one partner has been divorced. The family of the previously unmarried person tends to view the marriage with mingled hope and fear for the future, whether or not the fears are justified. The family of the divorced person cannot help but make comparisons between the new choice and the former mate. The fact that there was a previous marriage and a divorce will impact all relationships with family and former friends, even though the new couple feel that "all that is in the past."

Children. If the previous marriage has produced children, there are additional complicating factors. If the divorced parent has visitation rights, the new spouse must adjust to having the children around on days when they visit. The parent will have to contact the former partner to arrange these visits. The parent may have a financial responsibility for the children. Few men earn enough money to adequately support two families. The new partner may have to help her mate meet financial obligations to a first family.

The divorced person may be less tolerant of difficulties the second time around. A divorced person is more susceptible to divorce again. Second marriages have a higher divorce rate than first marriages. And in our society today there is little stigma connected to divorce, so when serious problems arise, a person who has divorced before may choose divorce again as a solution. Something happens the second time around. Could it be that a pattern of running from problems instead of facing them is established? There is also the possibility that the divorced person is a relatively unmarriageable type or a difficult marriage type (even though you may not yet have seen these hidden traits).

If you are considering marriage to a divorced person, be alert in evaluating his personality and adjustability. Realize that, statistically speaking, the divorced person is a greater marriage risk than one who has not been previously married, and the divorced woman is an even greater risk than the divorced man.

> *In 1969 an eighty-two-year-old woman and an eighty-two-year-old man married in Mexico City. They had been engaged for sixty-seven years!*
>
> The Incomplete Book of Failures

Divorced people have a higher rate of marriage failure because they (1) tend to marry divorced persons; (2) have less hesitation to divorce a second time, since the barriers against it have broken down (according to the National Center for Health Statistics, divorced people seek divorce an average of two years sooner than first timers); (3) may habitually try to escape from problem situations rather than work through them; (4) may have hurt so badly from the trauma of divorce that they compensated by rebounding rapidly into a new love experience. This last point may be the most important. Studies show that divorced people tend to remarry quickly after a divorce, the large majority remarrying within two years, and they remarry after shorter acquaintance and with shorter engagements (often with no engagement period at all) than do people who are entering their first marriage. When divorced people divorce again, it is usually after a shorter marriage than the first time. It seems to me that there should be a law requiring counseling before remarriage.

When considering marriage to a divorced person, one should contemplate how much the divorced individual has learned from his marriage failure. Does the person feel totally blameless, that it was all the mate's fault? If so, it is doubtful that such an individual is a good prospect for marriage. Those who have failed once should learn from experience and pinpoint areas in themselves that demand improvement. It is possible to learn through bitter experiences how to make a better choice the second time around and work more effectively at building a successful relationship. Ask yourself: What has this person learned that might have helped the first marriage succeed and that will make our marriage better?

Whenever a person marries, she is not marrying just one person but the intended's family as well. You may not be welcomed with open arms. Her parents may be retired or elderly. You may think of them as sweet old things who can't lift a finger to cause trouble, but think again.

Usually the new partner's mother causes more trouble than the father. If your partner has never been married before, the mother can be quite possessive and jealous. She may feel you are taking away the child she has enjoyed all these years. If you have been married before, she may see you as undeserving of her wonderful child and possibly as a wicked divorcée. If you've not been married before, she'll wonder why no one wanted you.

Move slowly. Try hard. Be nice. If you can't win the early battles, back off and be patient. Never stand in the way of family relationships. If it becomes a war, it may be that your partner will have to visit his parents without you. If you do have the good fortune to marry into a family who adores you, reciprocate with gratitude. Such acceptance is a rare commodity in second marriages.

265

Wise Words for Widows and Widowers

Dealing with the loss of a partner through death is often simpler than dealing with a partner who is alive and still on the scene. A widow or widower can make decisions regarding children without interference from a former spouse. A divorced person can't. Decisions must be checked out with the other parent. Widows and widowers have to deal with grief but grief heals in time. What widows and widowers need to avoid is marrying too soon. The average person works through the normal stages of grief in two to seven years. But those who are still working through grief and attempting to build a new love relationship at the same time will run into major problems at some point. The widow or widower has good potential for becoming a great marriage partner, but the grief over death of a spouse must be overcome first. As one man who had been married within a year of his beloved wife's death said to me, "I'm crawling the walls. I feel like I am riding down two separate tracks at the same time."

If you have been widowed and are contemplating a relationship with a new person, slow the relationship down. You can't build a new love relationship and bury the dead simultaneously. Bury the dead first. Attend a grief seminar and make sure you move through the stages of grief. Then slowly and surely take your time in building a new relationship. Start with friendship and move on up through the stages, taking two full years—even if you are sixty-eight years old. It's better to spend quality years together than to rush into marriage and regret it the rest of your years.

Can Blending Bring Mending?

A leading family authority has stated that stepparenting is five times more difficult than any other kind of parenting! The most confused, angry, bitter, and uncooperative families I encounter are those who are trying to blend "his kids," "her kids," and sometimes "their kids." In one particular instance a troubled family came for help. The new stepfather blamed the family's unhappiness on his wife's sixteen-year-old daughter. Angrily he growled, "I married her, not her daughter!" When one marries a parent with minor children, it's a package deal. The children come with the parent.

One study of two thousand stepchildren, most of whom came from divorced homes, found a greater amount of "stress, ambivalence, and low cohesiveness" in their families than in first-marriage families. The study also pointed out that it was more difficult to be a stepmother than a stepfather and that stepdaughters had more trouble adjusting to the new family than stepsons. Obviously a stepmother must work harder at developing cohesive relationships.

Children between the ages of twelve and eighteen present the most challenging problems. Very young and college-age children adjust more easily, with six- to twelve-year-olds falling somewhere in between. But whatever the age, parenting his, hers, and their children presents unusual challenges.

The parent and stepparent must have a united front. That means they must discuss their expectations for the children to be sure they coincide. Once agreed, both parents should discuss matters with the children so the children get a clear message that the stepparent is part of the permanent "team."

Even though behavior expectations may have been discussed prior to marriage, parents can expect opposition from the children. During the first few years after remarriage, children tend to recognize only the natural parent's right to discipline. The children test and retest the limits set by the stepparent. This is part of a child's need to explore the limits of any new relationship or situation. The sooner the stepparent makes her presence felt and shows the child she is there to stay, the sooner the child will accept the reality that her former family is gone (either through divorce or death) and accept the new parent. Be patient during the adjustment process. Most authorities agree that it takes two to three years for the average child to work through the stages of recovery after the loss of a parent, and some are now saying seven years.

In a home where there has been no divorce and remarriage, either parent can resolve problems created by a child and administer punishment when it is called for. If the punishment is unfair, the child generally forgives readily whether or not the parent asks for forgiveness. But not so in the blended family. Instead, the stepparent questions his own right to discipline, the natural parent questions whether the stepparent is being fair, and the child questions the stepparent's attempt to control her.

> *To marry once is a duty, twice a folly, thrice is madness.*
>
> Great Thoughts,
> Funny Sayings

Stepparents should mentally prepare themselves for possible initial feelings, on the part of the child, of resentment rather than love. It is important to remember that the child has already sustained a loss through death or divorce—a loss that makes her extremely vulnerable to hurt. The child has just come through an emotionally devastating time, which affects her behavior and frequently causes her to act worse than she normally would. The stepparent often misinterprets the misbehavior to be a rejection of her when this may not be the case. The stepchild who visits on occasion may never love the stepparent in the real sense of the word. Someone has suggested that the word *love* should be stricken from the stepparent's vocabulary. Instead, the stepparent should seek to form with the child a relationship of respect that may, with time, blossom into affection.

No one can force a child to love a stepparent. But both parents can make the child understand that even though the stepparent is not the real parent, she will be carrying out all the functions of a parent, and whether the child loves the new parent or not, the child must obey. This will take courage and strength on both parents' parts, but the more consistently it is done, the stronger the family relationship will become. It may seem unlikely but it's true that stepparents build relationships with stepchildren most easily when the children are on good terms with their natural parent.

Becoming the stepparent to the child of a divorce may be very different from stepparenting a child who yearns for someone to fill the void left by a parent who died. The longer the child has lived in the single-parent home after the death of the parent, the more rigid his memories become and the more difficult the adjustment to a stepparent. The child will likely expect the new parent to take up where the old one left off, which isn't possible.

Every child in the newly formed family should feel a part of the family as soon as possible. The child needs to know he has a special place. Even if the stepchild visits only on weekends or holidays, it is still necessary to arrange a place that belongs only to him—a bed, a drawer, certain possessions. In the blended family where two sets of children are merged, providing each child his own space becomes even more important. One mother who moved her two children into the home of her new husband and his two children said, "All the children have been forced to do some adjusting. The children must share bedrooms. My oldest daughter wants a bedroom of her own, and my husband's children are whining, 'Whose house is this, anyhow?'"

The entire stepfamily needs to find common ground. It may be a fun activity or a sharing of jobs that can bring them together. Weekend camping, a sport enjoyed by all, a love for bird watching, and participating in church activities together can help family members bond. This type of activity will help the family members become friends.

A happy blended family is possible where the adults are mature, patient, and persistent, and where the love of God is consistently demonstrated during and beyond the blending process. Always remember, however, that the most important relationship is the one between husband and wife, not between parent and child. When the husband-wife relationship is at its best, the parent-child relationship has a better chance of succeeding.

Remarriage in Later Years

Len had been married for twenty-two years to the same wife when she died of cancer. Theirs was a good relationship. When they had a problem, they talked it out. Now Len is alone and feels lost. A short time after his wife's death he met Beth. Intense loneliness urged him to remarry quickly.

He told a friend, "I can't bear being alone. I can't deal with it emotionally. Beth and I get along pretty well. I think I'll marry her. Anything would be better than the way I'm feeling now." Shortly after the wedding Len and Beth found out how little they knew about each other. Len needed someone to soothe his intense loneliness. He expected Beth to care for him just as his previous wife had done. Beth wasn't interested in that type of life. She wanted their pre-wedding fun to continue—dinners out, long drives in the country, picnics, and all the attention he had showered on her. She needed someone to take her out and entertain her. Both realized too late they had married too quickly.

Working through grief does not mean rushing into a new relationship to dull the pain or selling your house to escape past memories. Nor does it mean taking a trip to forget. These are all escape mechanisms. Both men and women need to work through grief, but men have a tendency to remarry sooner. After the loss of a partner, men need someone to take care of them as well as a companion.

A man who remarries within two years of the death of his spouse wants a wife to prepare meals, make their home comfortable, plan the social life, be hospitable to his family and friends, as well as carry financial responsibility and activities with her own family and friends. He may also want her to contribute financially to their home, clothes, and medical care.

After the loss of a partner a woman usually wants a man to date. She wants to be taken out for dinner. She needs affection.

One good unwritten rule for widowed or divorced people is that they should make no major change in their lives, such as selling a house, for at least a year, to be sure of using good judgment. Moving means a loss of familiar surroundings and may adversely affect self-image. This is especially true for the female who created the home. The loss of a partner creates enough stress without moving, which is also stressful. It is comforting to stay in the same home with the warm memories.

Both men and women must complete their mourning before even thinking about remarriage. For a man, this is usually about two years. Women need almost twice as long. Before deciding to marry again, a wise couple will see each other for a period of at least two years, under many varied situations, not just pleasant dates. Then they should take another couple of years before marriage to work out business, legal, and family issues. This is all very complicated. You may decide it isn't worth it to remarry. And it just might be the best decision you ever made.

Four Trouble Spots for Those over Fifty

A million people over fifty remarry every four years in the United States. There are four important concerns that people over fifty must consider before remarrying.

Adult Children

"Every child opposes a second marriage for his or her parents," according to Dr. Stanley Heller, a distinguished psychiatrist. "The structure of the family has changed. One parent is missing. A new person is there. Particularly if there is an estate, children resent having to share it with a stranger. They also resent having to share a parent, or feel disloyal to the departed parent."[6]

One of the greatest joys of a first marriage is children. In later years they remain the main source of emotional support in stress, illness, old age, and death. But in a second or third marriage, one or more of the adult children and their spouses often cause trouble. This may come as a shock to a newly married older couple. According to Dr. Heller the problem usually stems from adult children who feel they did not get enough love when growing up.

One newly married couple in their sixties got a rude awakening two months after their wedding. Adult children from both previous marriages came to the home. The husband's children created a terrible scene over something the new wife had done. The wife's children rose to her defense. Her husband said and did nothing, and she felt that he had abandoned her.

Such situations are not uncommon. Some adult children accept the new relationship. Some never do. Visits can be filled with hostility and extremely stressful. After a holiday visit from his children, one man said, "I can't believe my children are acting this way."

Children of widows and widowers over sixty have trouble accepting a new wife due to inheritance concerns. Even when financial matters have been carefully spelled out in a will, money still causes trouble. The issue is feelings, not facts.

An important reason adult children do not accept a new spouse is because they have not completed their mourning for the deceased parent. As I've said, this takes a minimum of two years. The thought of their mother or father marrying again causes them pain, and they react. After two years, adult children should be more accepting of the courtship of a parent. Then if the parent spends two more years getting to know the person, it will not only strengthen the upcoming marriage, but also strengthen the new partner's relationship with the adult children.

Sometimes it becomes necessary for mothers in a second marriage to see their adult children separately from their spouse. One woman rents a condo near the ocean for herself and her children. For two weeks she, her children, and grandchildren are together while her husband stays home and plays golf.

Money and Estate Concerns

A widow must be aware she will lose entitlement to her deceased husband's Social Security benefits if she remarries before age sixty. She will also probably lose, on remarriage, some or all of her widow's benefits from her deceased husband's retirement plan. If she signs a prenuptial agreement, she may also lose that portion of the estate of her husband-to-be, usually one third or more, which most states grant a widow.

There are many ways to handle finances when you have been in one marital relationship and are forging a new one, but flexibility and good judgment are important. You may want to consult a Christian financial counselor.

Here again adult children who are concerned with wills, estates, and money can cause problems. Carefully talk through every monetary issue with each other, and don't assume anything.

Inflexible Living Habits

People who remarry bring much baggage with them—children, money, material possessions, homes, routines, and habits. In later life most persons are not as flexible about change as they were earlier in life. Habits and patterns of doing things become entrenched over the years. When two people in later life are trying to merge their lives, each is bound to find in the other personal habits that are distasteful. Since both have become more set in their ways, the habits they don't like in the other will cause increasing stress. This factor needs careful examination prior to marriage. Examine each other's habits and be honest with yourself about your ability to live with them. Assume that you won't be able to change them and then be ready to adapt after marriage.

Aging

Health and retirement concerns must be considered by those over fifty. If both partners are in good health, lead active lives, and practice good health habits, they can probably enjoy some good years together. But both must recognize that after sixty, some health problems will probably develop and a health problem for either could greatly alter their lifestyle.

In general, however, those who remarry in their fifties do so at a good age. Children are out of the nest, both have energy to enjoy life, and their sex life should be strong and comforting. Both husband and wife are working. The jolt of retirement hasn't hit.

> *Harry Stevens of Wisconsin is the oldest bridegroom on record. In 1984, the 103-year-old Stevens married 84-year-old Thelma Lucas.*
>
> The Wrong Stuff

In sharp contrast, being in one's sixties seems to be the most difficult age to begin a new marriage. This seems to be the decade of the greatest predictable change. Retirement is near or has taken place. The male sex drive varies dramatically, but a woman's desire continues. Health changes occur, and there is less energy.

274

Those who marry in their seventies have accepted the inevitable changes that later life brings and may marry for companionship. Anyone marrying in their eighties risks caring for a sick spouse.

Remarriage later in life can work if several steps are taken in advance. The first thing is to allow yourself enough time to heal from either death of a spouse or divorce. It is important to sort out the issues involved so that you can go into a new marriage wisely. Many concerns need to be addressed before you set a wedding date. Jane Hughes Barton in _Remarriage after Fifty_ doesn't mince words when she says: "Wait at least four years, but preferably longer, before remarrying, just to make sure you're marrying for the right reasons."[7]

The Last Word

D on't let yesterday use up too much of today. The past is past. You did the best you could with the knowledge you had at the time. To whip yourself mercilessly with endless guilt or to blame others for what happened will not solve anything; it will only hinder your growth process.

Whatever your mistakes, God will accept you where you are and set you free from the load you are carrying. God always deals with us as we are today, now, not yesterday or three years ago. Today you have a fresh opportunity to approach Him and go forward in faith. Paul talks about "forgetting what lies behind and reaching forward to what lies ahead" (Phil. 3:13 NASB). Focus your eyes, heart, and mind on Him. Allow Him to work in your life today.

An item in a church bulletin read: "Spiritual growth class postponed until September." Spiritual growth is not something that can be put off. Either we are progressing or regressing. Remember, the world is round, and the place that seems like the end may be only the beginning. Venture forth with new determination to rebuild your life with what you have, in keeping with God's plan.

Through Christ you can have a hope for the future that goes beyond the broken dreams, promises, and hurt you may have experienced. Through Jesus you can obtain a vision of your potential if you gain the courage to face the

276

problem—to begin to risk, to start over again. Remodeling may require growing pains, but look to the Master Architect for the finished product.

There is a second chance. With God's help, you can build a future that will weather the storms of life triumphantly! He can help you build a relationship that will last a lifetime.

One of the big challenges for adult singles is trying to avoid the potholes of life. All of us face life's potholes, but single people must dodge them alone. Trying to escape all of them would be like attempting to dodge every pothole on the Long Island Expressway in April. Another tactic might work better and is succinctly summed up by Portia Nelson:

Autobiography in Five Short Chapters

I

I walk down the street.
There is a deep hole in the sidewalk.
I fall in.
I am lost . . . I am helpless.
It isn't my fault.
It takes forever to find a way out.

II

I walk down the same street.
There is a deep hole in the sidewalk.
I pretend I don't see it.
I fall in again.
I can't believe I am in the same place.
But it isn't my fault.
It still takes a long time to get out.

III

I walk down the same street.
There is a deep hole in the sidewalk.

I see it is there.
I still fall in . . . it's a habit.
My eyes are open.
I know where I am.
It is my fault.
I get out immediately.

IV

I walk down the street.
There is a deep hole in the sidewalk.
I walk around it.

V

I walk down another street.

It's possible that another street also has a pothole—so beware. You are making choices daily that can lead to love, happiness, and fulfillment or to another pothole. Choose wisely!

Notes

Chapter 1: *Prerequisite for Love*

1. Nathaniel Branden, "A Woman's Self-Esteem," *New Woman* (Jan. 1993), 56–58.
2. Ibid.

Chapter 2: *Improving Your Self-Image*

1. Branden, "A Woman's Self-Esteem," 56–58.
2. Ron Lee Davis, *Mistreated* (Portland: Multnomah, 1989), 84–86. Used by permission.

Chapter 3: *How the Thirty-to-Sixty-Something Crowd Plays the Game*

1. Neil Clark Warren, *Finding the Love of Your Life* (Colorado Springs: Focus on the Family, 1992), 9.

Chapter 4: *Great Dates*

1. Jacqueline Simenauer and David Carroll, *Singles: The New Americans* (New York: Simon & Schuster, 1982), 19.
2. Ibid., 33.

Chapter 5: *Facing Reality*

1. Warren, *Finding the Love of Your Life*, 117–28.
2. Family Information Services, "Healthy Alternatives to Relationships for Teens—Breaking the Cycle of Violence in Family and Dating Relationships" (Sept. 1990), 48.
3. Ibid., 49.

4. The term BTN originated with Susan Page in *If I'm So Wonderful, Why Am I Still Single?* (New York: Viking, 1988), 80.

Chapter 6: *Ending It*

1. Simenauer and Carroll, *Singles*, 119.
2. Barbara de Angelis, *How to Make Love All the Time: Secrets for Making Love Work* (New York: Rawson), 257–60.

Chapter 7: *True Love*

1. James Dobson, *Love Must Be Tough* (Waco, Tex.: Word, 1983), 41.
2. Joyce Brothers, *The Brothers System for Liberated Love and Marriage* (New York: Peter H. Wyden, 1972), 19.
3. Ibid.
4. Ibid.
5. Ibid., 22.
6. John James and Ibis Schlesinger, *Are You the One for Me?* (Reading, Mass.: Addison-Wesley, 1987), 198.
7. Joyce Brothers, "Men in Love and Marriage," *Woman's Day* (Jan. 12, 1982), 43.
8. "Love styles" are adapted from H. Norman Wright, *Holding On to Romance* (Ventura, Calif.: Regal, 1992), 69–78.

Chapter 8: *Love or Infatuation*

1. This section adapted from Wright, *Holding On to Romance*, 75–77.

Chapter 9: *Touchy Situations*

1. Susan Crain Bakos, "The Sexually Assertive Woman," *Ladies Home Journal* (May 1992), 152, 203.
2. Gail L. Zellman et al., "Misreading the Signals," *Psychology Today* (Oct. 1980), 112.
3. Simenauer and Carroll, *Singles*, 151–52.

Chapter 10: *Pair Bonding*

1. Donald M. Joy, *Bonding: Relationships in the Image of God* (Dallas: Word, 1985).
2. For further information about double bonding and how to keep a bond strong, see chapter 2, "Pair Bonding: Pathway to Intimacy," in Nancy Van Pelt, *How to Talk So Your Mate Will Listen and Listen So Your Mate Will Talk* (Grand Rapids: Revell, 1989).
3. Joy, *Bonding*, 41.
4. Ibid., 44–45.

Chapter 11: *Abstinence*

1. McManus, *Marriage Savers*, 92.
2. Ibid., 65.

3. Diane Hales, "The Facts of Love," _Ladies Home Journal_ (March 1995), 66–69.

4. Mark Clements, "Sex in America Today," _Parade_ (Aug. 7, 1994), 5.

5. Erica Lumiere, "Women and AIDS," _Ladies Home Journal_ (Sept. 1995), 44.

6. As cited in "How AIDS Can Be Spread," _Message_ magazine supplement (June 1991), 24–25. Adapted from Jeanne Blake, _Risky Times_ (New York: Workman Publishing, 1990).

7. Marianne K. Hering, "Believe Well, Live Well," _Focus on the Family_ (Sept. 1994), 4.

8. Ibid.

9. Ibid. Michael J. McManus is quoted after appearing on the _Focus on the Family_ radio program.

10. Bryan Strong and Christine De Vault, _The Marriage and Family Experience_, 3rd ed. (San Francisco: West, 1986), 223. Also see Ira Reiss, "A Multivoiate Model of the Determinants of Extra Marital Sexual Permissiveness," _Journal of Marriage and Family_ (May 1986), 395–411.

11. Max Lucado, _No Wonder They Call Him the Savior_ (Sisters, Ore.: Multnomah, 1993), 43–45.

12. Jessica Synder Sachs, "Perimenopause: The Changes before the Change," _New Woman_ (Nov. 1994), 46.

13. Debra A. Bell, "Helping Women Overcome Abortion Effects," _Virtue_ (Jan./Feb. 1988), 10.

14. Eugene J. Kanin and David H. Howard, _American Sociological Review_ 23, no. 5: 558.

Chapter 12: _God's Plan for Sex_

1. Jim Talley and Bobbie Reed, _Too Close Too Soon_ (Nashville: Thomas Nelson, 1982).

2. Jim Talley, _Too Close Too Soon Workbook_ (Nashville: Thomas Nelson, 1984), 16.

3. Jeannie Park and Vicki Sheff-Cahan, "Oh, What a Night," _People_ (April 1992), 108–14.

Chapter 13: _Getting Fit to Be Tied_

1. Laura Schlessinger, _Ten Stupid Things Women Do to Mess Up Their Lives_ (New York: Harper Perennial, 1995), 91–92.

2. Michael J. McManus, _Marriage Savers_ (Grand Rapids: Zondervan, 1993), 36.

3. Schlessinger, _Ten Stupid Things Women Do_, 92.

4. Glenn T. Stanton, "Guess What—God Knows Best," _Focus on the Family_ (Aug. 1995), 2–4.

5. Sue Browder, "Is Living Together Such a Good Idea?" _New Woman_ (June 1988), 120–24.

6. Ibid.

7. McManus, _Marriage Savers_, 124.

8. *Prepare-Enrich, Inc.,* P.O. Box 190, Minneapolis, MN 55440.

9. Psychological Publications, Inc., 5300 Hollywood Blvd., Los Angeles, CA 90027.

Chapter 14: *Second Chances*

1. Bruce Fisher, *When Your Relationship Ends* (Boulder, Colo.: Family Relations Learning Center, 1978), 58.

2. Jim Smoke, *Growing in Remarriage: Seven Keys to a Successful Second Marriage* (Grand Rapids: Revell, 1990), 130.

3. Melinda Blau, "After Divorce," *New Woman* (May 1992), 82.

4. Smoke, *Growing in Remarriage,* 24.

5. *Ladies Home Journal* (Nov. 1985), 80.

6. Ann Doss Helms, "Making a Match after 50 Can Be a Messy Affair," *Fresno Bee* (March 6, 1995), F1.

7. Jane Hughes Barton, *Remarriage after Fifty: What Women, Men, and Adult Children Need to Know* (Fort Walton Beach, Fla.: Thomas Press, 1994).

Bibliography

Barton, Jane Hughes. *Remarriage after Fifty: What Women, Men, and Adult Children Need to Know.* Fort Walton Beach, Fla.: Thomas Press, 1994.

Bhaerman, Steve, and Don McMillan. *Friends and Lovers: How to Meet the People You Want to Meet.* Cincinnati: Writer's Digest Books, 1986.

Brenton, Myron. *Lasting Relationships.* New York: A & W Publishers, 1981.

Brothers, Joyce. *The Brothers System for Liberated Love and Marriage.* New York: Peter H. Wyden, 1972.

Bustanoby, André. *Being a Single Parent.* New York: Ballantine Books, 1985.

———. *The Ready-Made Family.* Grand Rapids: Zondervan, 1982.

Cabot, Tracy. *Marrying Later, Marrying Smarter.* New York: McGraw-Hill, 1990.

de Angelis, Barbara. *Are You the One for Me? Knowing Who's Right and Avoiding Who's Wrong.* New York: Delacorte, 1992.

———. *Secrets about Men Every Woman Should Know.* New York: Delacorte, 1990.

Dobson, James C. *Love Must Be Tough.* Waco, Tex.: Word, 1983.

Dominitz, Ben. *How to Find the Love of Your Life.* Rocklin, Calif.: Prima, 1986.

Fields, Doug, and Todd Temple. *Creative Dating.* Nashville: Thomas Nelson, 1986.

Gosse, Richard. *Looking for Love in All the Right Places.* Saratoga, Calif.: R & E Publishers, 1985.

Grant, Toni, *Being a Woman: Fulfilling Your Femininity and Finding Love.* New York: Random House, 1988.

Hendrix, Harville. *Keeping the Love You Find.* New York: Pocket Books, 1992.

Hybels, Bill and Lynne. *Fit to Be Tied.* Grand Rapids: Zondervan, 1991.

James, John, and Ibis Schlesinger. *Are You the One for Me? How to Choose the Right Partner.* Reading, Mass.: Addison-Wesley, 1987.

Kent, Margaret. *How to Marry the Man of Your Choice.* New York: Warner Books, 1987.

Kuriansky, Judy. *How to Love a Nice Guy.* New York: Doubleday, 1990.

Lasswell, Marcia, and Norman N. Lobsenz. *Styles of Loving: Why You Love the Way You Do.* Visalia, Calif.: Doubleday, 1980.

McDowell, Josh. *The Secret of Loving.* Wheaton, Ill.: Tyndale, 1985.

McManus, Michael J. *Marriage Savers.* Grand Rapids: Zondervan, 1993.

McShane, Claudette. *Warning! Dating May Be Hazardous to Your Health.* Racine, Wisc.: Mother Courage Press, 1988.

Page, Susan. *If I'm So Wonderful, Why Am I Still Single?* New York: Viking, 1988.

Purnell, Dick. *Becoming a Friend and Lover.* San Bernardino: Here's Life Publishing, 1986.

———. *Building a Relationship That Lasts.* San Bernardino: Here's Life Publishing, 1988.

Rinehart, Stacy and Paula. *Choices.* Colorado Springs: Navpress, 1982.

Rouner, Arthur A. *Struggling with Sex.* Minneapolis: Augsburg, 1987.

Rue, Nancy N. *Coping with Dating Violence.* New York: Rosen, 1989.

Schlessinger, Laura. *Ten Stupid Things Women Do to Mess Up Their Lives.* New York: Harper Perennial, 1995.

Simenauer, Jacqueline, and David Carroll. *Singles: The New Americans.* New York: Simon & Schuster, 1982.

Smoke, Jim. *Growing in Remarriage: Seven Keys to a Successful Second Marriage.* Grand Rapids: Revell, 1990.

Stafford, Tim. *Love, Sex, and the Whole Person.* Grand Rapids: Zondervan, 1991.

Sydnor, Rebecca. *Making Love Happen.* New York: British American Publishing, 1989.

Talley, Jim A., and Bobbie Reed. *Too Close Too Soon.* Nashville: Thomas Nelson, 1982.

Van Pelt, Nancy L. *The Compleat Courtship.* Hagerstown, Md.: Review and Herald Publishing, 1982.

―――. *How to Talk So Your Mate Will Listen and Listen So Your Mate Will Talk.* Grand Rapids: Revell, 1989.

Warren, Neil Clark. *Finding the Love of Your Life.* Colorado Springs: Focus on the Family, 1992.

Wright, H. Norman. *Holding On to Romance.* Ventura, Calif.: Regal, 1992.